Making Books with Pockets

The series of monthly activity books you've been waiting for!

Enliven every month of the year with fun, exciting learning projects that students can proudly present in a unique book format.

Each month has lessons for art, writing, reading, math, science, social studies, and poetry.

Michelle Barnett, Caitlin Rabanera, and **Ann Switzer** have taught first, second, and third grade. Their teaching experiences have involved working with limited-English-speaking students from many parts of the world, supervising student teachers, and conducting inservice sessions for colleagues. They are currently teaching in Southern California.

Congratulations on your purchase of some of the finest teaching materials in the world.

For information about other Evan-Moor products, call 1-800-777-4362 or FAX 1-800-777-4332
Visit our website http://www.evan-moor.com. Check the Product Updates link for supplements, additions, and corrections for this book.

Authors:	Michelle Barnett
	Caitlin Rabanera
	Ann Switzer
Editors:	Marilyn Evans
	Jill Norris
Copy Editor:	Cathy Harber
Illustrator:	Jo Larsen
Designer:	Cheryl Puckett
Desktop:	Shannon Frederickson

Entire contents ©1999 by EVAN-MOOR CORP.
18 Lower Ragsdale Drive, Monterey, CA 93940-5746.
Permission is hereby granted to the individual purchaser to reproduce student materials in this book for noncommercial individual or classroom use only. Permission is not granted for schoolwide, or systemwide, reproduction of materials.
Printed in U.S.A.

Evan-Moor
EDUCATIONAL PUBLISHERS
EMC 586

W9-AGQ-218

March's Special Days

Here are ideas for celebrating some of the other special days in March.

March 1 _____ **National Pig Day**
Talk about famous pigs with your class. Read *Pigs* by Robert Munsch.

March 2 _____ **Dr. Seuss's Birthday**
Read any one of Dr. Seuss's stories. Have students tell their favorites. Make up your own silly rhyming Dr. Seuss-like story for a class book.

March 3 _____ **Hina Matsuri (Doll Festival)**
In Japan special dolls are passed from generation to generation. On this day these special dolls are displayed on steps covered with red cloth. Families and friends visit each other to admire the dolls and share tea and cookies. Celebrate Hina Matsuri by inviting students to bring a special doll or figurine to class. Cover a display area with red cloth or paper. Let students take turns telling about their special doll or figurine.

March 11 _____ **Johnny Appleseed Day**
Bring in apples of all shapes and colors for everyone to enjoy.

March 19 _____ **The swallows return to Mission San Juan Capistrano**
Locate San Juan Capistrano, California, on a map. How far from your city is this?

March 21 _____ **First Day of Spring**
Make a list of things that spring: grasshoppers, rabbits, frogs, a spring, kangaroos, etc.

All Month _____ **National Noodle Month and National Peanut Month**
Cook noodle dishes from many different cultures, pattern with colored noodles for a math lesson, and create mosaics with noodles.

Read about how peanuts grow, learn the many uses for peanuts invented by George Washington Carver, and, of course, make peanut butter and chant the old favorite "Peanut Butter, Peanut Butter—Jelly, Jelly." (Evan-Moor's theme unit *From Farm to Table*, EMC 551, has a minibook and other activities on peanut butter.)

March

Sunday	Monday	Tuesday	Wednesday	Thursday	Friday	Saturday

How to Make Pocket Books

Each pocket book has a cover and three or more pockets. Choose construction paper colors that are appropriate to the theme of the book. Using several colors in a book creates an effective presentation.

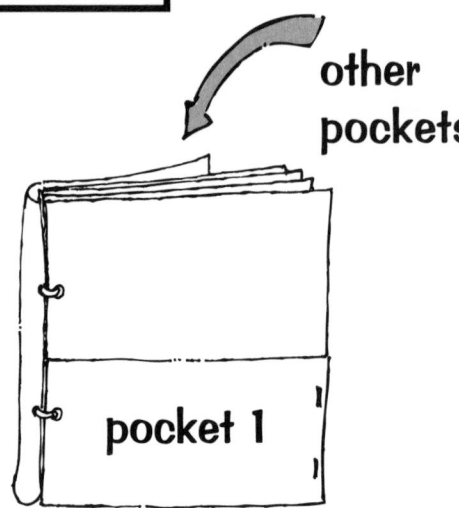

other pockets

pocket 1

Materials

- 12" x 18" (30.5 x 45.5 cm) piece of construction paper for each pocket
- cover as described for each book
- hole punch
- stapler
- string, ribbon, twine, raffia, etc., for ties

Steps to Follow

1. Fold the construction paper to create a pocket. After folding, the paper should measure 12" (30.5 cm) square.

2. Staple the right side of each pocket closed.

3. Punch two or three holes in the left side of each pocket and the cover.

4. Fasten the book together using your choice of material as ties.

5. Glue the poem or information strips onto each pocket as shown on the overview pages of each book.

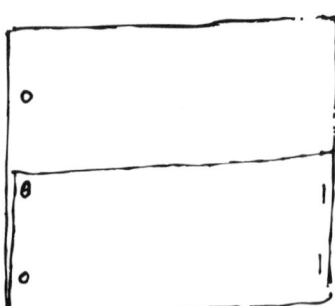

St. Patrick's Day

This happy holiday book is built around a St. Patrick's Day poem. Students will experience art, oral and written language, and math.

The poem can also be used for pocket chart activities throughout the month:
 • Chant the poem
 • Listen for rhyming words
 • Learn new vocabulary
 • Identify sight words
 • Put words or lines in the correct order

Use the picture dictionary to introduce new vocabulary and as a spelling reference. Students can add new pictures, labels, and descriptive adjectives to the page as their vocabulary increases.

Use this form for story writing or as a place to record additional vocabulary words.

BIBLIOGRAPHY

Clever Tom & the Leprechaun by Linda Shute; Scholastic, 1988.

Fortunately by Remy Charlip; Aladdin, 1993.

Jamie O'Rourke and the Big Potato by Tomie De Paola; Scholastic, 1992.

Mary McLean & the St. Patrick's Day Parade by Steven Kroll; Scholastic, 1991.

Potato by Barry Watts; Silver Burdett Press (Stopwatch Books), 1987.

Saint Patrick and the Peddler by Margaret Hodges; Orchard Books, 1993.

Shamrocks, Harps, and Shillelaghs by Edna Barth; Clarion Books, 1977.

St. Patrick's Day by Gail Gibbons; Holiday House, 1994.

St. Patrick's Day in the Morning by Eve Bunting; Clarion Books, 1980.

Tim O'Toole and the Wee Folk by Gerald McDermott; Puffin Books, 1990.

POCKET 1

Rainbow and Pot of Gold   pages 9–11
Find our "pot of gold" at the end of this tissue paper rainbow that comes from a 3-D paper cloud.

Where Is the Pot of Gold?   pages 12–14
Students learn about prepositions by describing the positions of a pot of gold. Then they make a book with their own sentences that tell where the pot of gold is located.

POCKET 2

Mosaic Leprechaun   pages 15 and 16
All about Leprechauns   pages 17 and 18
Who doesn't recognize this sprightly symbol of St. Patrick's Day? Students will make a colorful mosaic leprechaun, learn about this Irish fairy, and then write their own fanciful leprechaun tales.

POCKET 3

Music of Ireland   **pages 19 and 20**
Read this minibook to learn about the harp, pipes, and fiddle.

Glittering Harp   **pages 21 and 22**
Adorn this pocket with a golden harp made from construction paper.

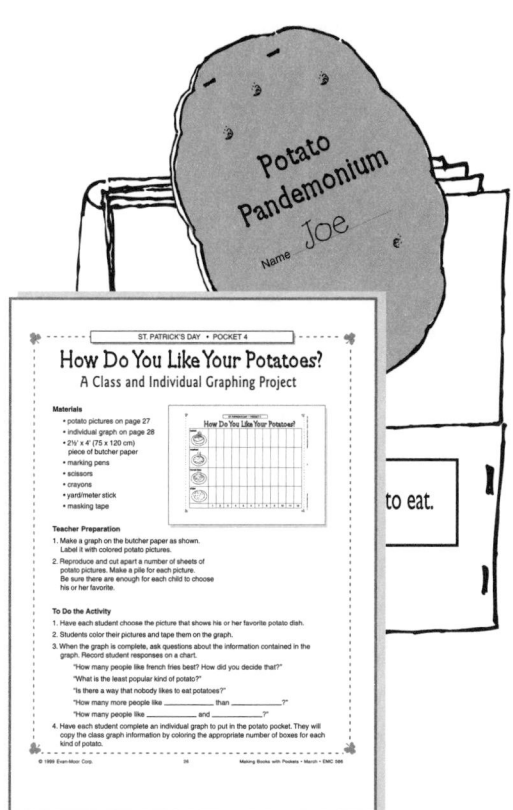

POCKET 4

Potato Pandemonium Book pages 23–25
Learn about why potatoes are associated with St. Patrick's Day and make a potato book.

**How Do You
Like Your Potatoes?**   **pages 26–28**
What kind of potatoes do your students like to eat? Make individual and class graphs to find out.

POCKET 5

Hidden Shamrock   **pages 29 and 30**
Create a shamrock from three hearts held together with a paper fastener. Then write a wish on the back of each leaf.

**Good Luck,
Bad Luck Book**   **pages 31 and 32**
Students make an accordion book following a format similar to *Fortunately* by Remy Charlip.

Note: Reproduce this cover decoration for students to color, cut out, and glue to the cover of their St. Patrick's Day books.

Happy St. Patrick's Day

Rainbow and Pot of Gold

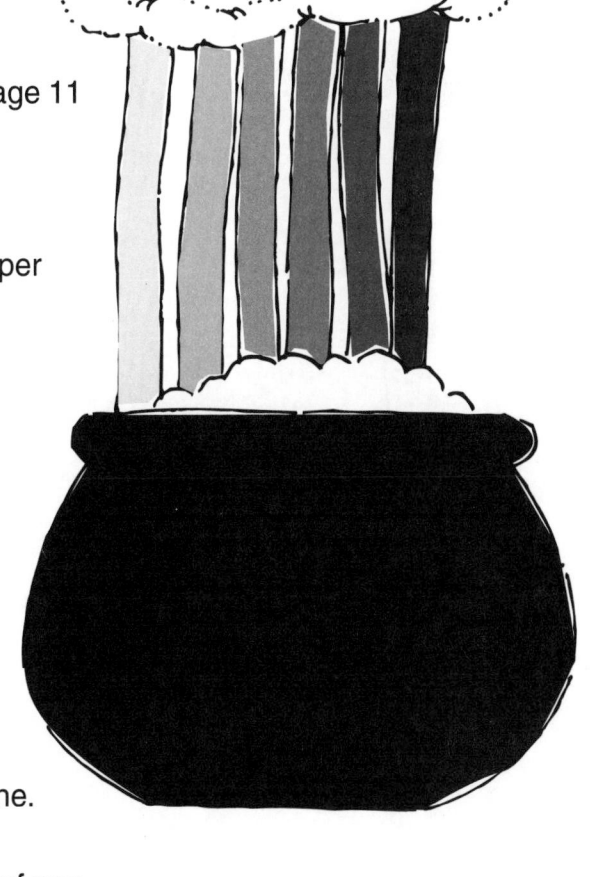

Materials

- 2 copies of the cloud pattern on page 10, reproduced on white construction paper
- tagboard pot templates, made from pattern on page 11
- construction paper
  pot–black, two 9" x 12" (23 x 30.5 cm) pieces
  gold–yellow, two 3" x 7" (7.5 x 18 cm) pieces
- 8" x 1" (20.5 x 2.5 cm) strips of colored tissue paper
- shredded newspaper
- yellow crayon or marker
- glue
- cotton balls
- 24" (60 cm) length of white yarn or roving
- hole punch

Steps to Follow

1. Using the pot template, cut 2 black pots.

2. Hold the two yellow pieces of paper together.
   Draw a scalloped line across the top. Cut on that line.
   Glue to the top of each pot.

3. Glue one end of the tissue paper strips to the back of one
   pot of gold. Glue the other end to the back of one cloud.
   Allow at least a 6" (15 cm) length of tissue paper to show.

4. Glue the other pot of gold to the first, sandwiching tissue
   strips in between the two pots.

5. Glue the two clouds together with tissue strips in between.
   Leave an opening along the top edge for stuffing with newspaper.

6. Stuff cloud with enough newspaper to make it look
   "fluffy" and then glue open edge closed.

7. Add cotton balls around the edge of the cloud to enhance its
   "billowy" look.

8. Punch a hole at the top and string a yarn loop for hanging.

Cloud Pattern

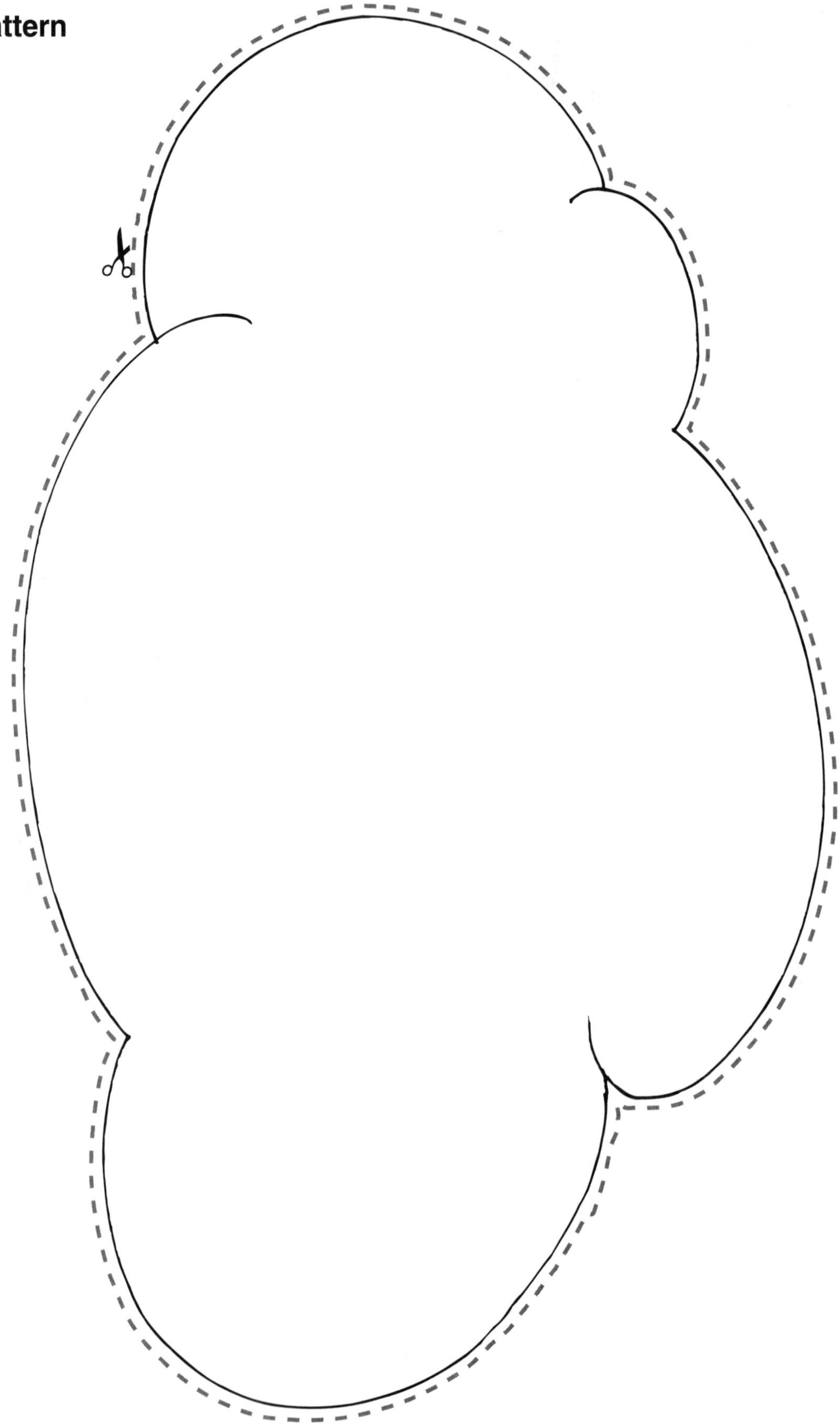

**Template for
Pot of Gold**

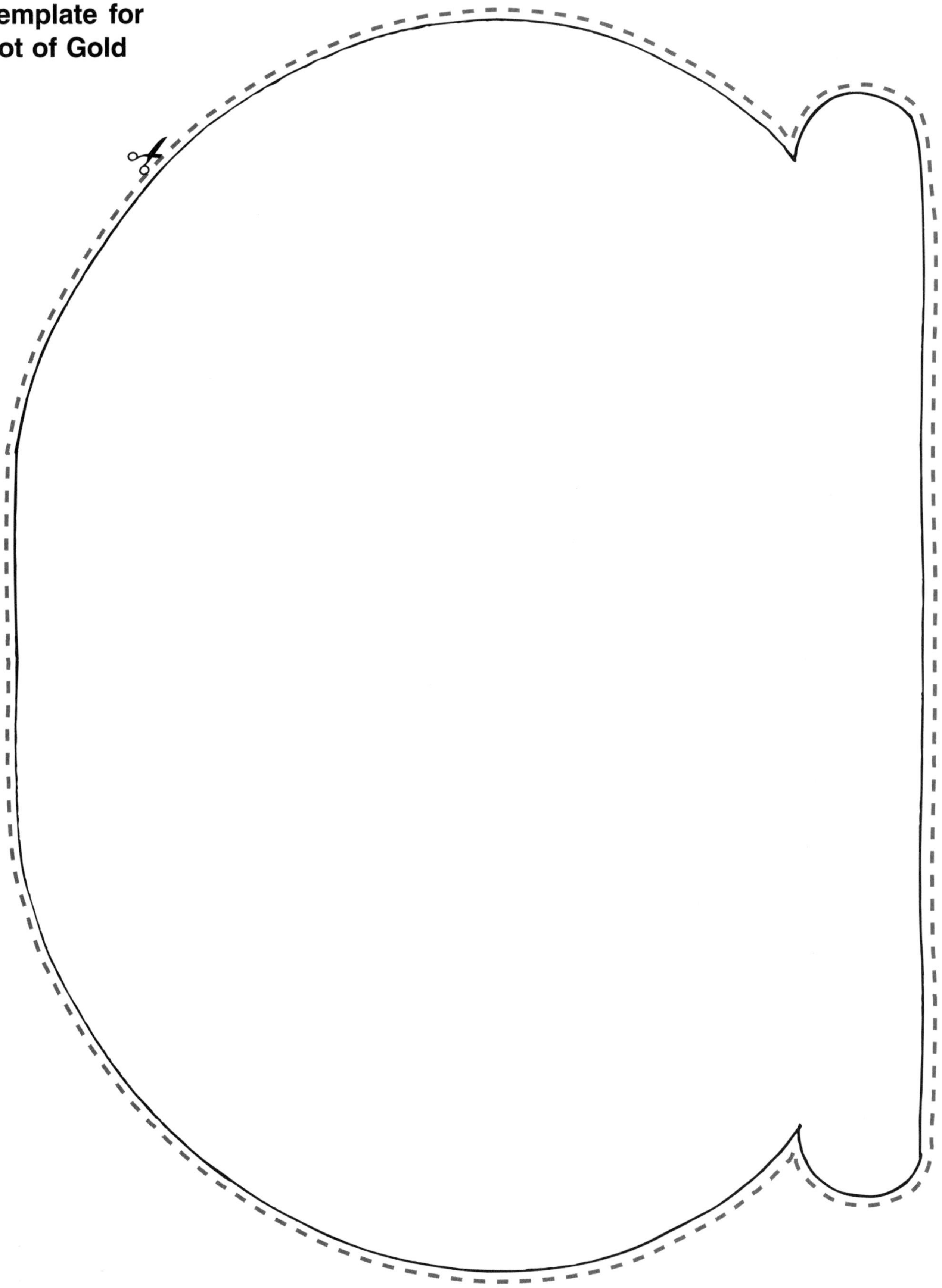

Where Is the Pot of Gold?
A Book about Prepositions

Materials

- pot template on page 13, reproduced on gray construction paper—2 per student
- writing form on page 14, several per student
- small scraps of yellow construction paper
- scissors
- crayons
- pencils
- "pot of gold"—can be any container
- optional: pieces of "gold"—candy coins, butterscotch pieces, etc.

Presenting the Lesson

1. Present your "pot of gold" to the class. Place it on a table. Ask, " Where is the pot of gold?" Write the phrase "on the table" on the chalkboard.

2. Move the pot of gold to various positions to elicit these prepositions: beside, above, behind, between, under, in front of, in back of, etc.

3. Explain that the list of words and phrases on the board all tell where something is located. Introduce the term *preposition* if it seems appropriate for your group.

4. Guide students to develop St. Patrick's Day-related sentences that use the prepositional words and phrases. Examples:

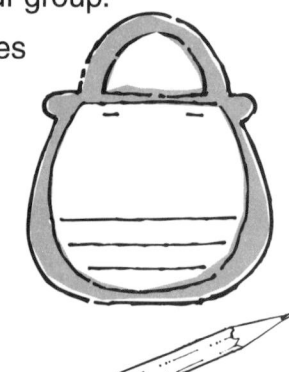

   The pot of gold is beside the leprechaun.

   The pot of gold is above the potato field.

   The pot of gold is between the mushrooms.

   The pot of gold is behind the harp.

5. On each writing form, students write a sentence that tells where the pot of gold is and underline the preposition used. Illustrate each sentence.

Making the Book

1. Cut out the two pots. Write the title "Where Is the Pot of Gold?" on one pot.

2. Tear "pieces of gold" from yellow paper scraps. Glue to the pot with the title.

3. Staple writing forms to the top edge of the second pot.

4. Glue the handles of the two pots together to form a book.

Pot Template

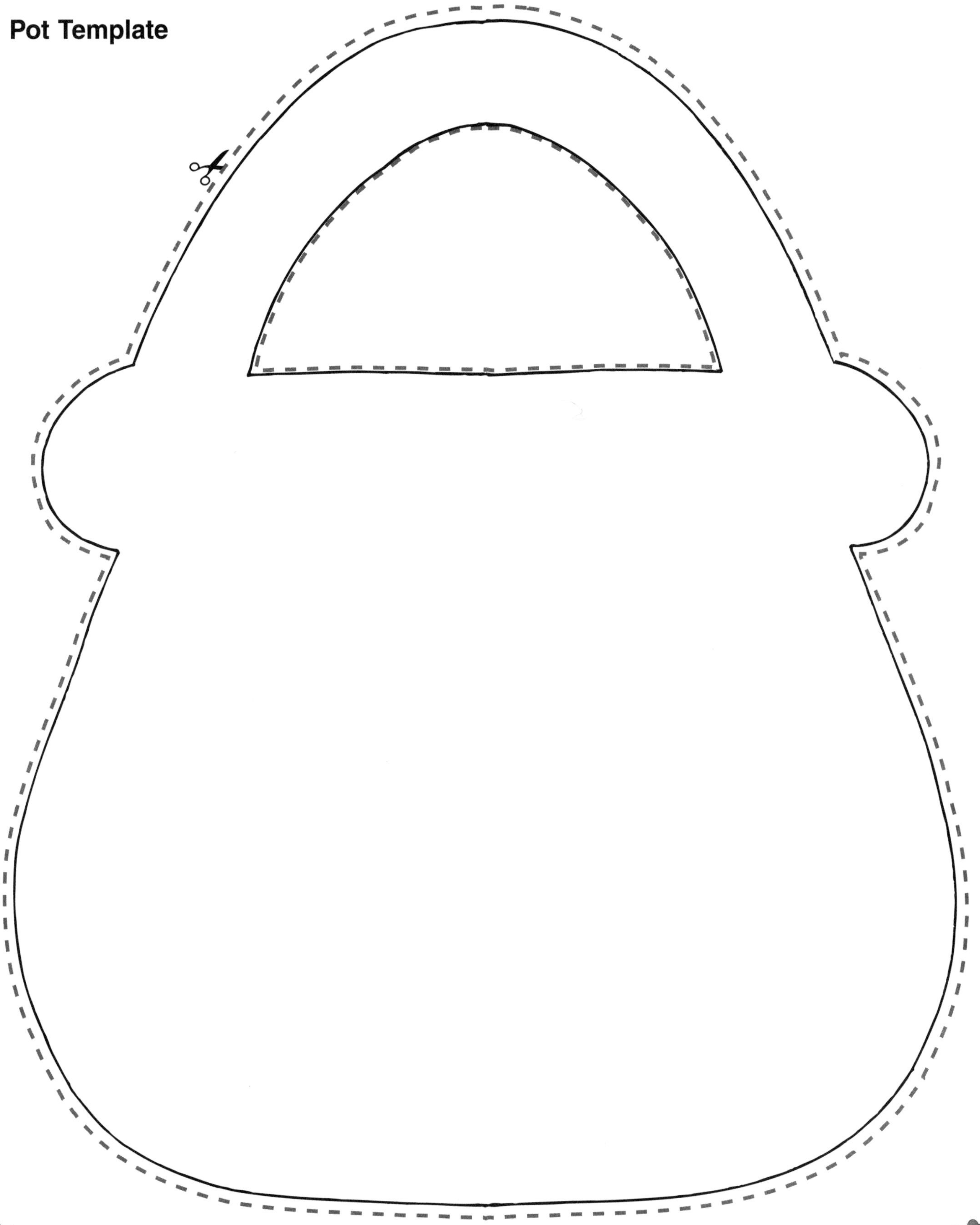

Pot Writing Form

Mosaic Leprechaun

Materials

- leprechaun face on page 16, reproduced on white construction paper
- dark green, light green, orange, and yellow construction paper cut into small squares and rectangles
- glue
- crayons

Steps to Follow

1. If your students have not done paper mosaic before, model the process for them:

   - Spread a thin layer of glue over a small section of the drawing.
   - Cover the glued area with overlapping paper pieces.
   - Repeat steps until the desired areas are completely covered.

2. Cover the leprechaun with paper pieces as follows:

   - yellow, dark green and light green pieces for the top of the hat
   - dark green pieces for the brim of the hat
   - orange pieces for the beard

3. Draw facial features on the leprechaun.

4. Cut out the leprechaun. (This can also be done before beginning the mosaic.)

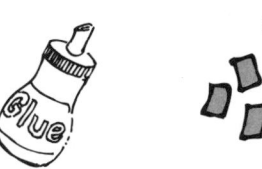

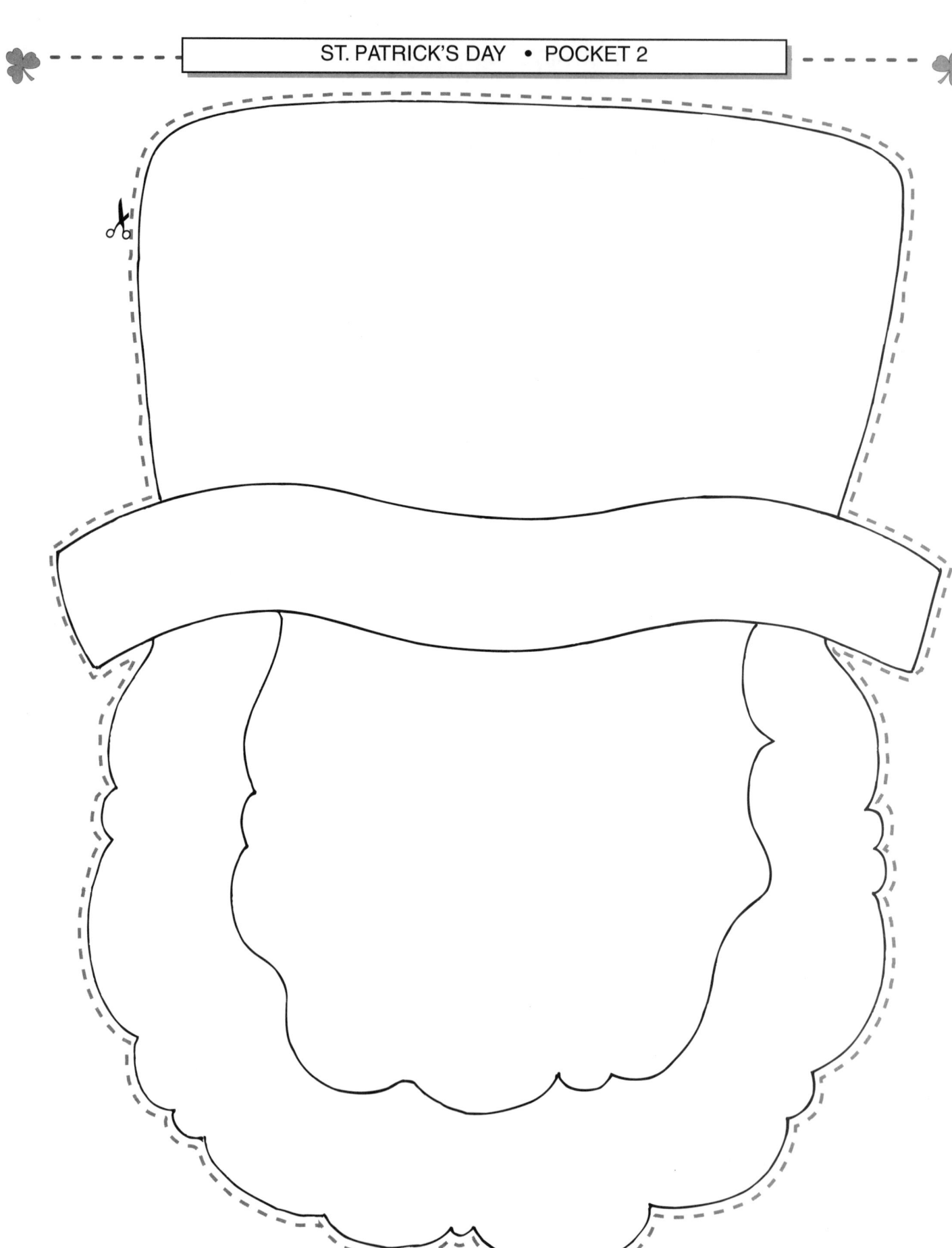

Making Books with Pockets • March • EMC 586

All about Leprechauns

- Read about leprechauns in *Shamrocks, Harps, and Shillelaghs* (see bibliography on page 5), or share the information provided here.

   There are two main types of Irish fairies. Trooping Fairies live and travel in groups and have kind dispositions. Solitary Fairies, like the leprechaun, live alone and are usually mean and spiteful.

   Leprechauns are teeny shoemakers that mend other fairies' shoes. Their favorite pastimes are music and dancing.

   Leprechauns are said to be rich and bad-tempered. They prefer to live far away from people. If caught, the captor has to keep a constant eye on the leprechaun or it will vanish. The leprechaun might attempt to buy his release by offering to take the captor to his hidden pot of gold. However, they are not trustworthy and always seem to escape without paying.

   Of all the Irish fairies, only leprechauns have a place in St. Patrick's Day celebrations. Maybe it's because a leprechaun's clothes are green.

- Read stories about St. Patrick's Day that feature leprechauns. As you read, keep a list of words that describe these wee folk—what they wear, how they look, how they act.

- Reproduce the writing form on page 18. Have students write a fanciful tale about a leprechaun. Brainstorm and list some titles to get ideas flowing. For example,
    "How I Caught the Leprechaun"
    "Why Leprechauns Dress in Green"
    "The Little People"
    "The Forgetful Leprechaun"
Encourage students to refer to the list of words about leprechauns as they write.

Name: _____

_____

Name: _____

Music of Ireland

Making Books with Pockets • March • EMC 586

The Irish harp is called the clarsach. It has been important in Ireland from earliest times. This small harp is held on the harpist's knee. The brass strings make a bell-like sound when they are plucked.

The harp is shown on Irish coins, the national coat of arms, and on some Irish flags.

Making Books with Pockets • March • EMC 586

The Irish love to dance to the music of the fiddle and the pipe.

© 1999 Evan-Moor Corp.   Making Books with Pockets • March • EMC 586

Here are some Irish musical instruments.

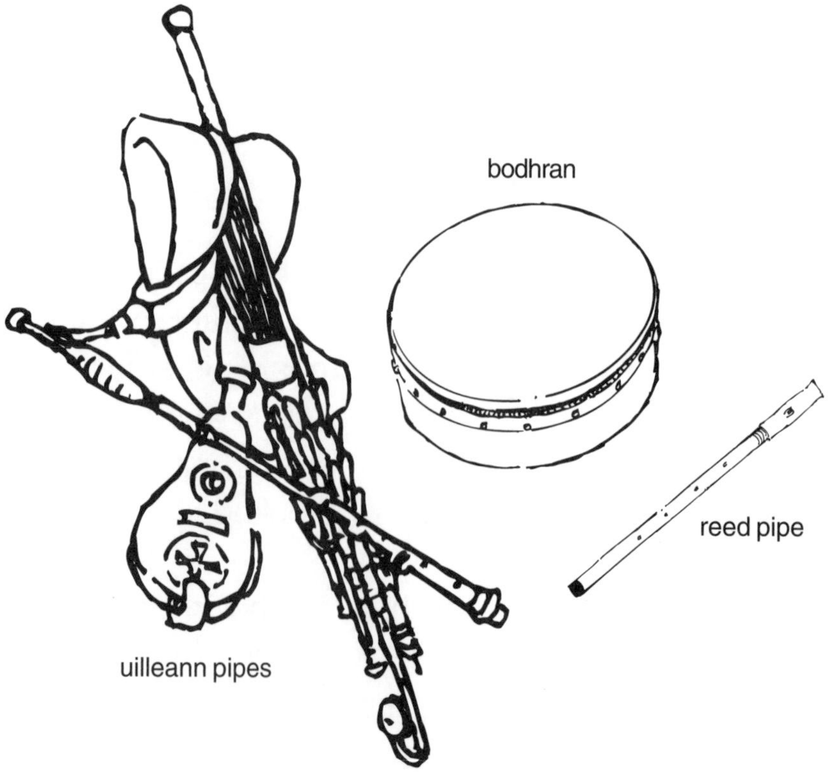

bodhran

reed pipe

uilleann pipes

© 1999 Evan-Moor Corp.   Making Books with Pockets • March • EMC 586

Glittering Harp

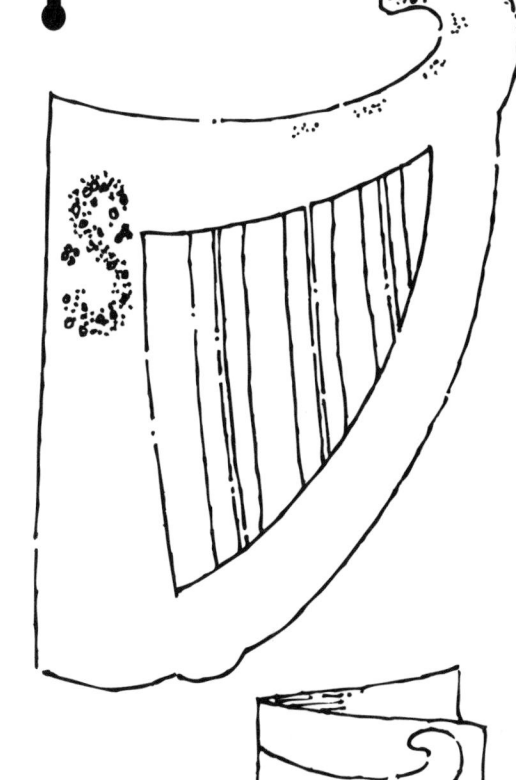

Materials

- tagboard harp templates, made from the pattern on page 22
- 12" x 18" (30.5 x 45.5 cm) yellow paper
- gold glitter
- six 6" (15 cm) pieces of string
- three ¾" x 6" (1½ x 15 cm) strips of white tissue paper
- glue
- scissors

Steps to Follow

1. Fold the yellow paper in half. Place the long edge of the harp on the fold and trace.

2. Cut out the harp; do not cut the fold.

3. Cut three strips of white tissue paper to fit vertically across the center of the harp, overlapping about ½" (1.25 cm) onto the yellow paper.

4. Glue string to each side of the tissue. Trim ends to adjust length where necessary.

5. Open the harp and glue the tissue/string pieces vertically across the center of the harp.

6. Glue the harp closed.

7. Use glue to create designs on the harp. Shake the gold glitter over the wet glue to add sparkle to your harp.

Harp Pattern

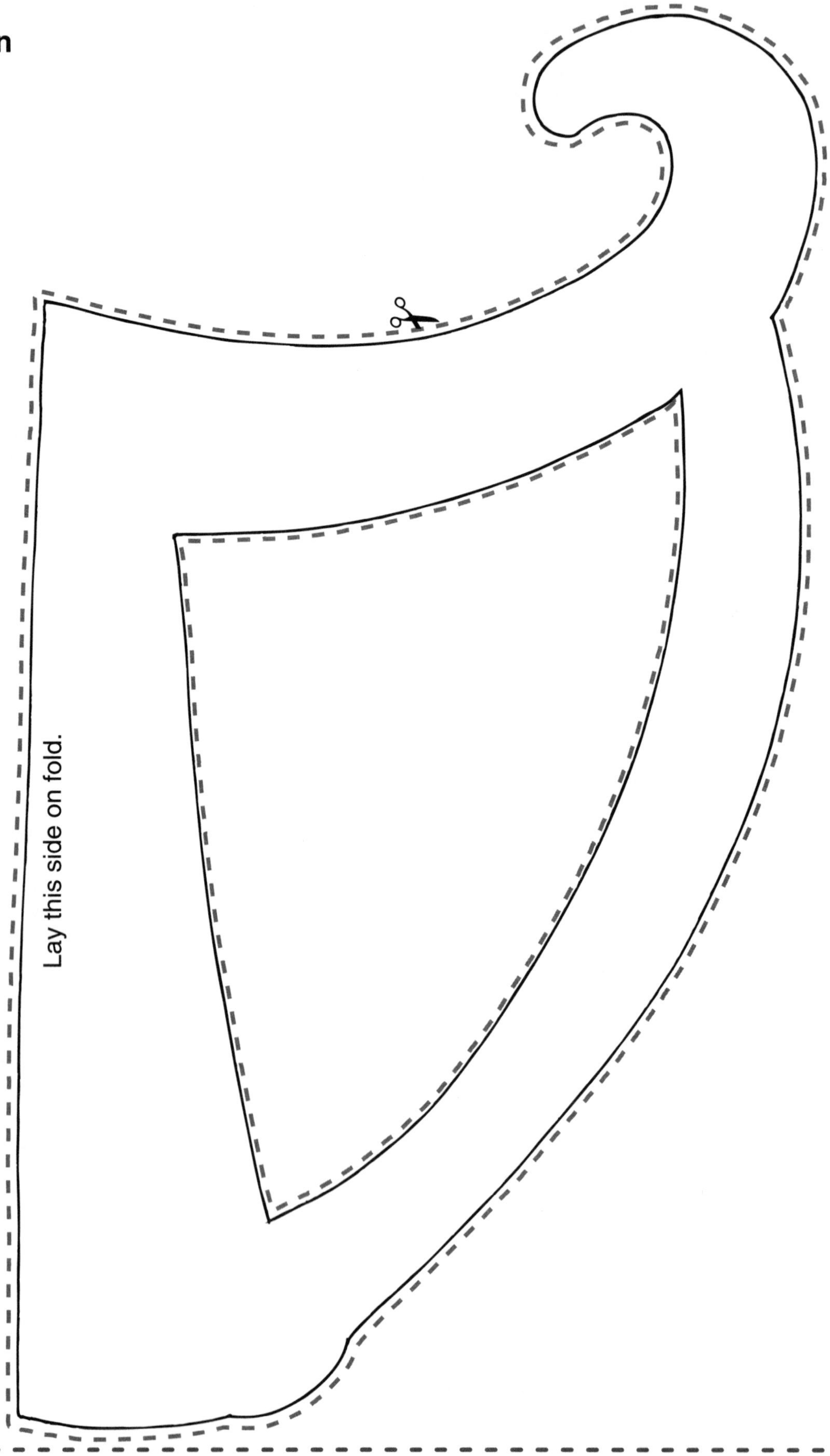

Lay this side on fold.

Potato Pandemonium

Read books about St. Patrick's Day and potatoes and then make a potato book using one or more of the writing activities suggested below.

- *Jamie O'Rourke and the Big Potato* by Tomie De Paola
- The section on potatoes from *Shamrocks, Harps, and Shillelaghs* by Edna Barth
- *Potato* by Barry Watts

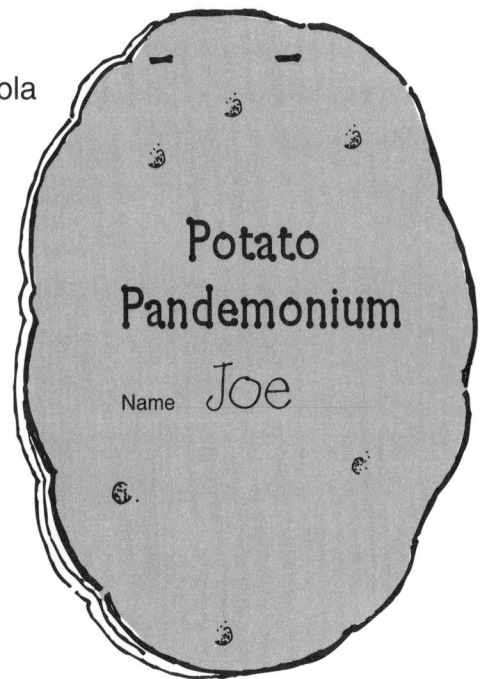

Materials

- cover pattern on page 24, reproduced on brown construction paper
- 5" x 7" (13 x 18 cm) piece of brown construction paper for back cover
- writing paper pattern on page 25
- scissors
- stapler

Steps to Follow

1. Cut out the front cover. Use it as a template to cut out the back cover.

2. Cut out the appropriate number of writing pages for the activity to be used. Place the writing pages between the covers and staple at the top.

Writing Ideas for the "Potato Pandemonium" book

1. Research potatoes and write potato facts, for example:

> They grow underground.
> The spots on a potato are called "eyes."
> Potato "eyes" are the "seeds" of the plant.
> In Ireland, potatoes are called "praties."

2. Research and write about the "Potato Famine" and the great immigration from Ireland to North America.

3. Write about all the different ways to prepare potatoes. Give a favorite potato recipe.

4. Grow a new potato plant and keep a journal of the growth.
   a. Stick toothpicks around the center of the potato.
   b. Place the potato in a glass jar with water. The toothpicks suspend the potato at the top of the jar, allowing only the bottom half to be submerged.
   c. Place near a window.

Cover Pattern

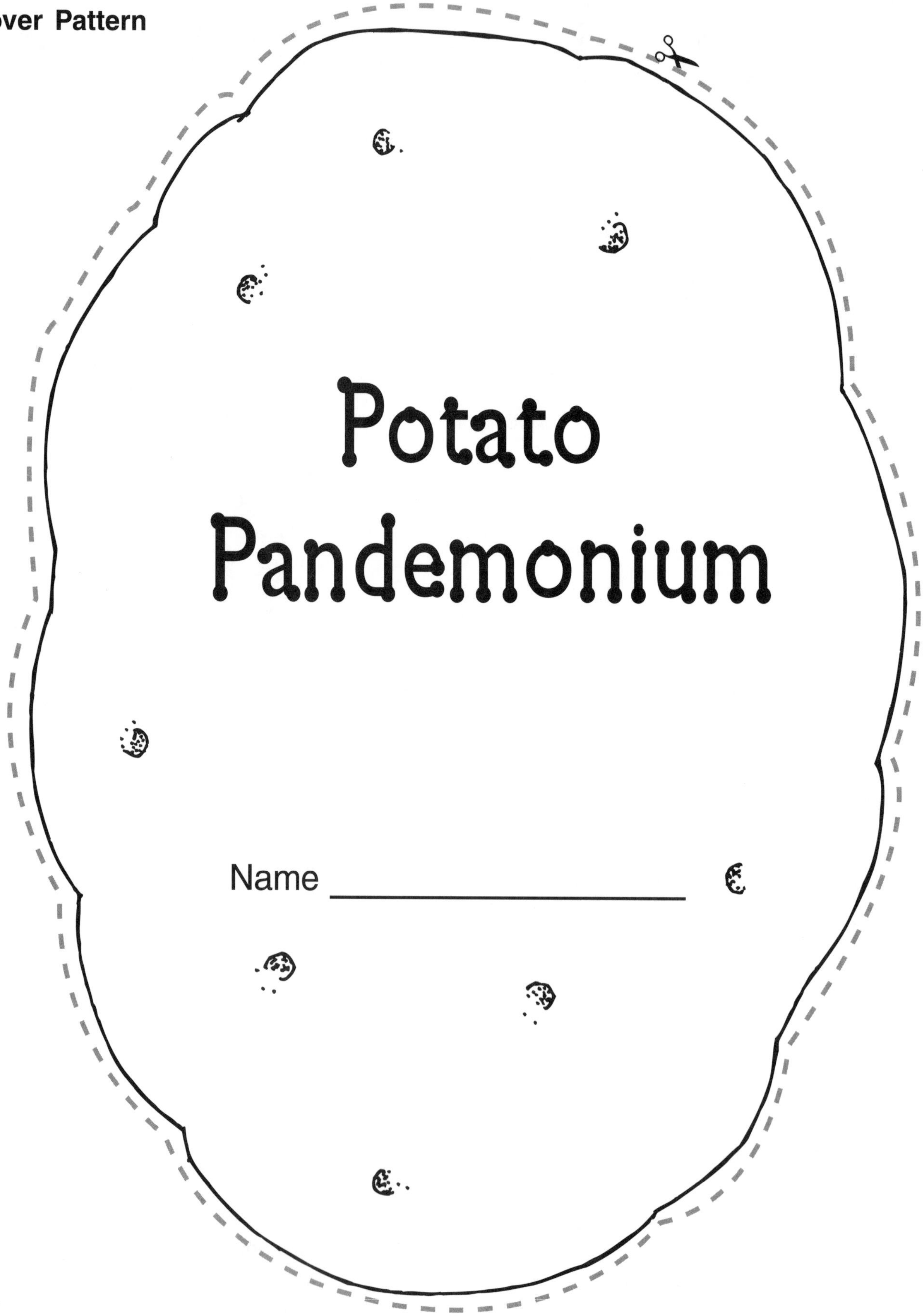

Potato Pandemonium

Name _____

Writing Form

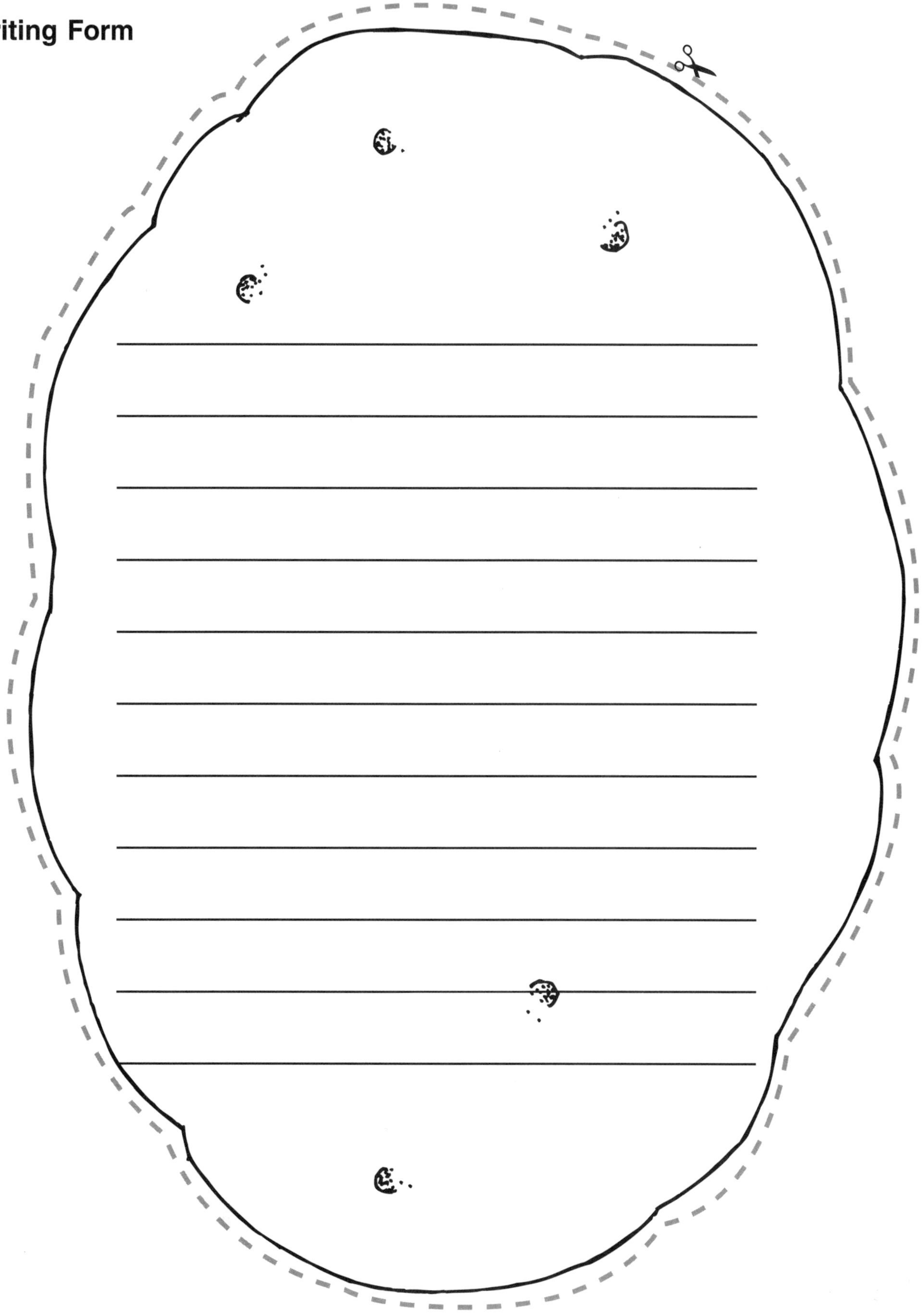

How Do You Like Your Potatoes?
A Class and Individual Graphing Project

Materials

- potato pictures on page 27
- individual graph on page 28
- 2½' x 4' (75 x 120 cm) piece of butcher paper
- marking pens
- scissors
- crayons
- yard/meter stick
- masking tape

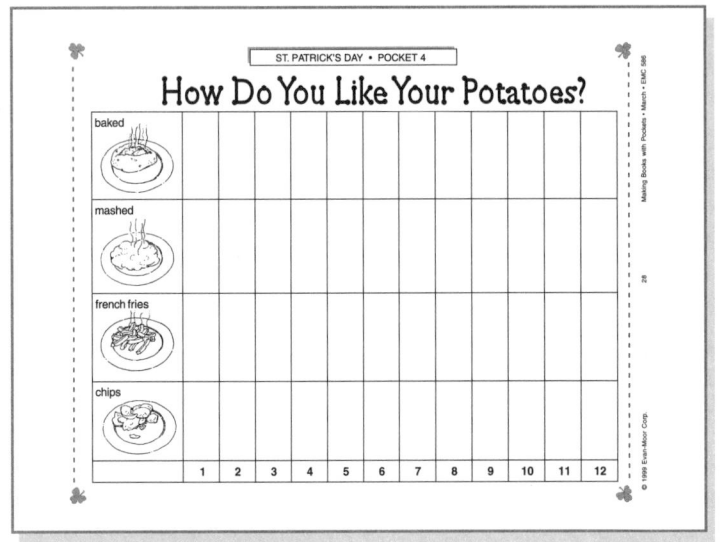

Teacher Preparation

1. On the butcher paper, make a graph similar to the one on page 28. Be sure to make the sections as large as the individual pictures on page 27. Label it with colored potato pictures.

2. Reproduce and cut apart a number of sheets of potato pictures. Make a pile for each picture. Be sure there are enough for each child to choose his or her favorite.

To Do the Activity

1. Have each student choose the picture that shows his or her favorite potato dish.

2. Students color their pictures and tape them on the graph.

3. When the graph is complete, ask questions about the information contained in the graph. Record student responses on a chart.

   "How many people like french fries best? How did you decide that?"

   "What is the least popular kind of potato?"

   "Is there a way that nobody likes to eat potatoes?"

   "How many more people like _____ than _____?"

   "How many people like _____ and _____?"

4. Have each student complete an individual graph to put in the potato pocket. They will copy the class graph information by coloring the appropriate number of boxes for each kind of potato.

Baked
Potatoes

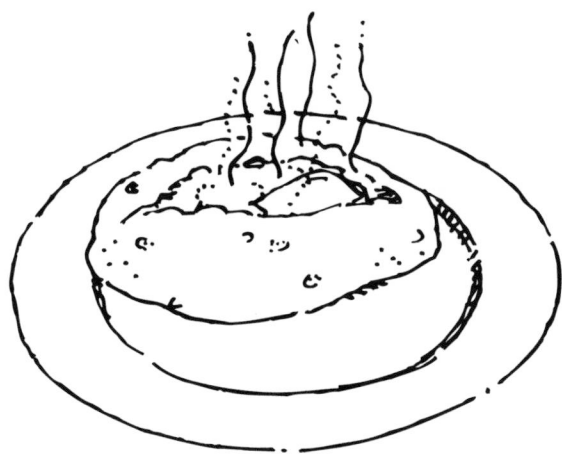

Mashed
Potatoes

French Fried
Potatoes

Potato
Chips

How Do You Like Your Potatoes?

	1	2	3	4	5	6	7	8	9	10	11	12
baked												
mashed												
french fries												
chips												

Hidden Shamrock

Before conducting the art lesson, share as much information about the shamrock as is appropriate for your students.

The shamrock has been associated with St. Patrick for centuries. Some say that the saint himself used the shamrock to explain the Christian concept of the Trinity. Later, the shamrock was an emblem of Irish regiments in the British army. The shamrock grows freely all over Ireland. Every March, millions of shamrock plants are shipped all over the world for St. Patrick's Day celebrations.

Materials

- pattern on page 30, reproduced on green construction paper
- paper fastener
- colored paper scraps
- markers
- crayons
- glitter
- sequins

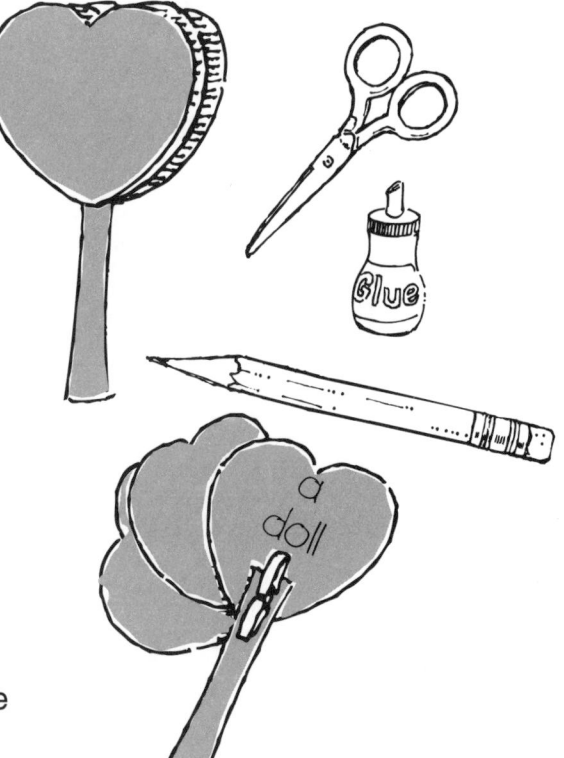

Steps to Follow

1. Cut out the three hearts to create leaves for the shamrock. Cut out a stem.

2. Decorate the hearts using crayons, paper scraps, glitter, or sequins.

3. Attach the bottom corner of each heart to the top of the stem with the paper fastener.

4. Push the stem and hearts together to make a single heart. Spread them apart to show the shamrock.

5. On the back of each leaf, have students write something they would wish for if they had a lucky shamrock.

Hidden Shamrock Pattern

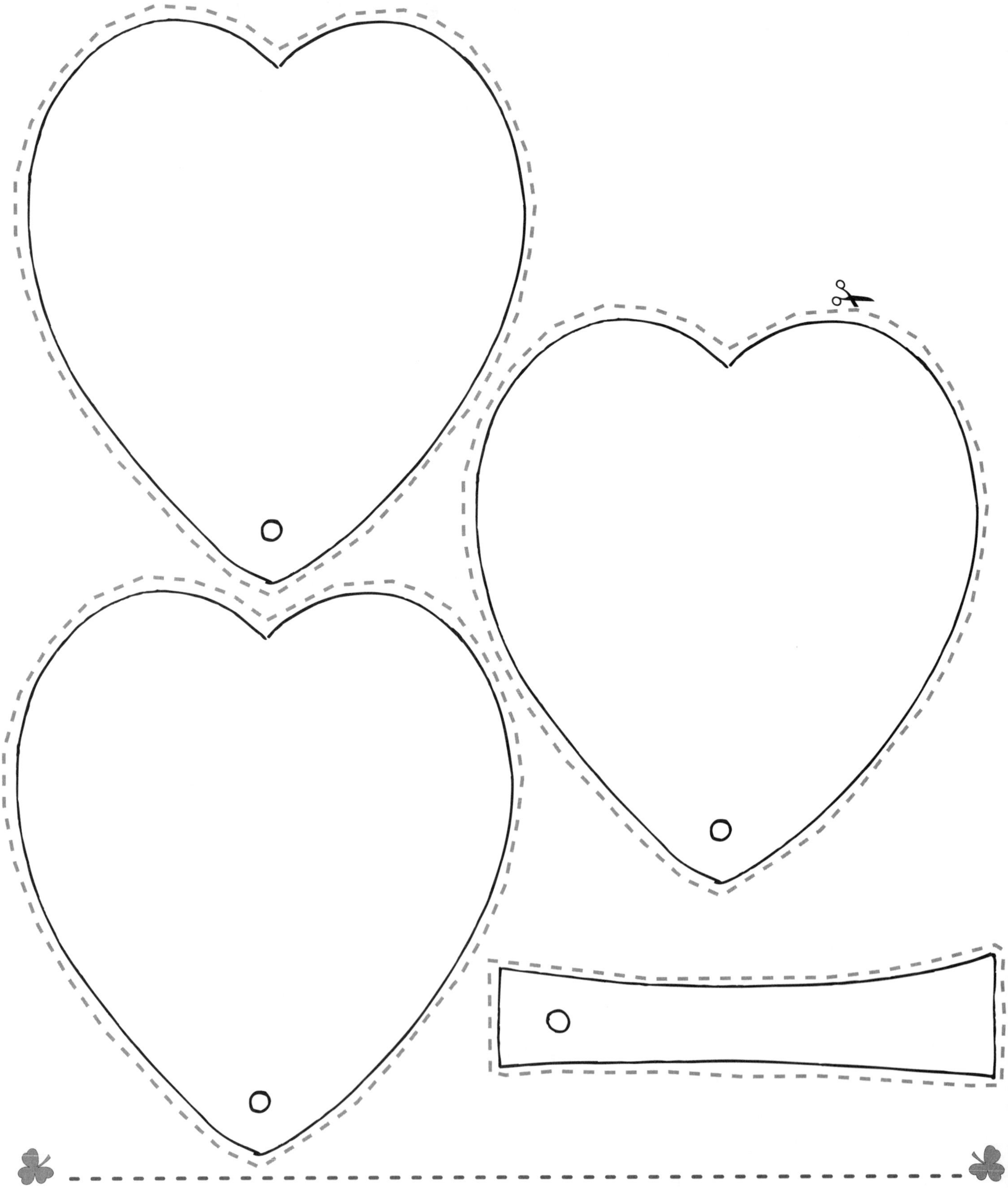

Good Luck, Bad Luck Book

St. Patrick's Day is full of symbols for luck—the shamrock, catching a leprechaun and being granted a wish, kissing the Blarney stone. The expression "The Luck of the Irish" implies that if you are Irish, luck is always with you. This lesson about good luck and bad luck uses a format similar to the book *Fortunately* by Remy Charlip.

Materials

- make a transparency of good luck symbols on page 32
- *Fortunately* by Remy Charlip
- 6" x 18" (15 x 48.5 cm) white construction paper
- glue
- crayons

Steps to Follow

1. Talk about symbols for luck, using the transparency.

2. Read the book *Fortunately*.

3. Have students create their own scenario using good luck and bad luck to create a "Good Luck, Bad Luck" book.

   - accordion-fold paper in thirds
   - write a good luck event in the first box and illustrate it
   - write a bad luck reaction to the first event in the second box and illustrate it
   - the last box should be a final good luck event

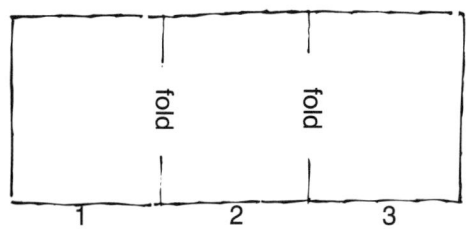

Good Luck Symbols

horseshoe

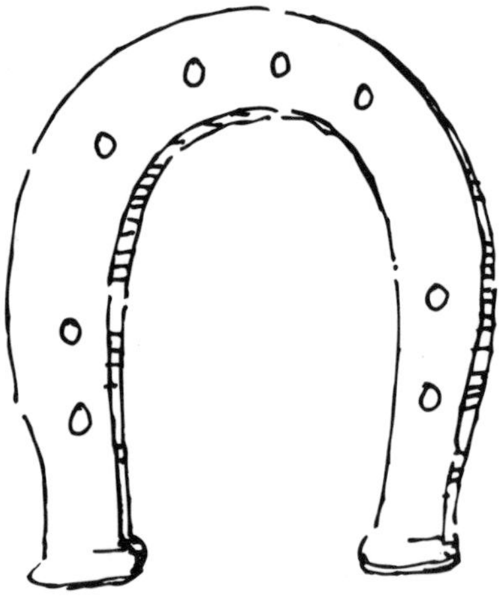

shooting star

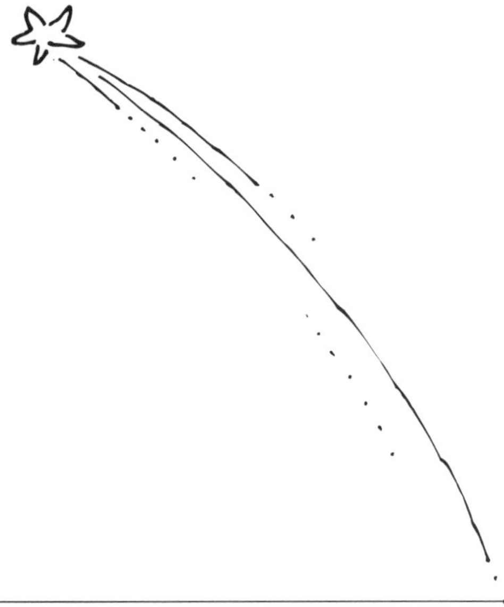

four-leaf clover

lucky penny

Note: Reproduce this page and page 34 to label each of the five pockets of the St. Patrick's Day book.

Pocket 1

Here is a rainbow with a pot of gold.

Pocket 2

Here is a leprechaun, tricky and bold.

Pocket 3

Here is a harp, a musical treat.

Pocket 4

Here is a potato, a favorite to eat.

Pocket 5

Here is a shamrock, a little green clover.

Happy St. Patrick's Day to you.

Make a wish before it's over!

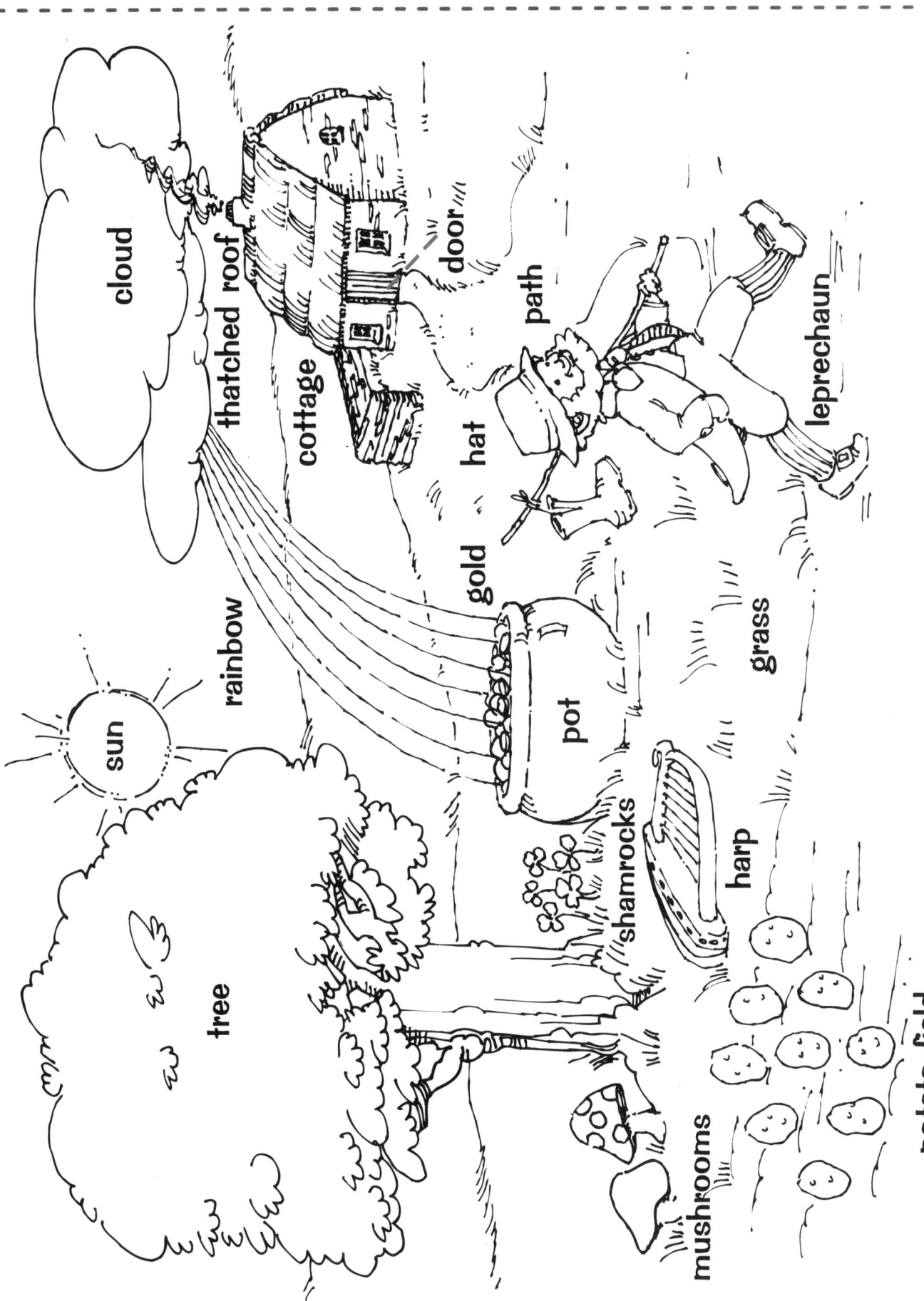

cloud

thatched roof

door

cottage

path

hat

gold

leprechaun

rainbow

sun

grass

pot

tree

shamrocks

harp

mushrooms

potato field

Making Books with Pockets • March • EMC 586

ST. PATRICK'S DAY WRITING FORM

Name: _____

_____

_____

_____

_____

_____

_____

_____

_____

_____

_____

_____

_____

_____

_____

_____

_____

_____

_____

_____

_____

Weather

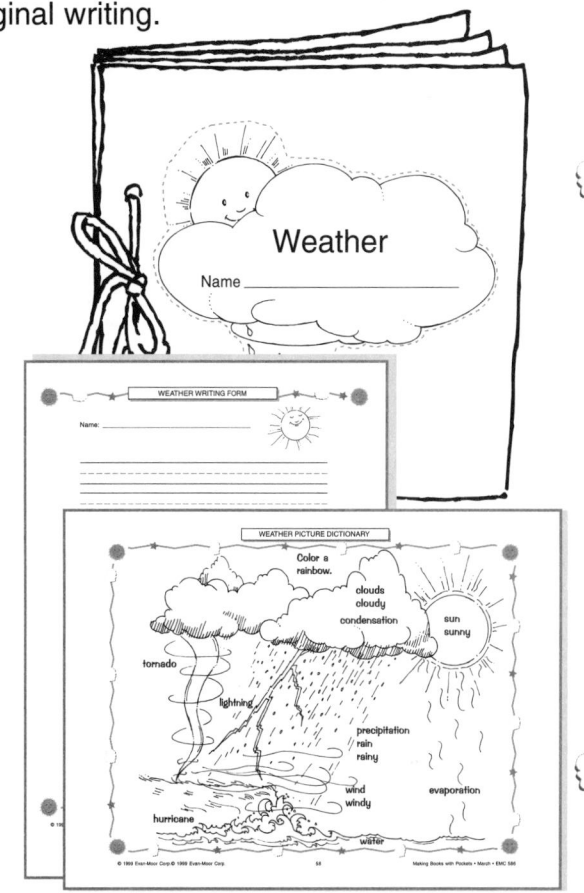

M arch is a month of volatile, changing weather patterns—blizzards, torrential rains, lots of wind to fly those March kites, and maybe even some gentle breezes and warm spring sunshine. The activities in this pocket book will enhance your science curriculum, as well as involve students in informational and original writing.

BIBLIOGRAPHY

The Cloud Book by Tomie de Paola; Scholastic, 1975.
A Drop of Water by Walter Wick; Scholastic, 1997.
Flash, Crash, Rumble, and Roll by Franklyn M. Branley; Thomas Y. Crowell, 1985.
Hurricane Watch by Franklyn M. Branley; Thomas Y. Crowell, 1985.
It Looked Like Spilt Milk by Charles G. Shaw; Harper Trophy, 1947.
Once Upon Ice by Jane Yolen; Wordson/Boyds Mills Press, 1997.
Rain Drop Splash by Alvin Tresselt; Scholastic, 1946.
Storms by Seymour Simon; Mulberry Books, 1989.
The Science Book of Weather by Neil Ardley; Harcourt Brace Jovanovich, 1992.
Tornado Alert by Franklyn M. Branley; Thomas Y. Crowell, 1988.
Water Dance by Tomas Locker; Harcourt Brace & Co., 1997.
Weather (an Eyewitness Book) by Brian Cosgrove; Alfred A. Knopf, 1991.
Weather by Gillimard Jeunesse; Scholastic, 1989.
Weather Words by Gail Gibbons; Scholastic, 1990.

Water Cycle

POCKET 1

Water Cycle Book   **pages 41–45**
After learning about the water cycle, students confirm their understanding by adding text to a minibook on the water cycle.

Types of Clouds

POCKET 2

Types of Clouds   **pages 46–48**
Learn about the main types of clouds through story, poetry, and by completing a follow-up worksheet.

A Cloud in a Jar   **pages 49 and 50**
Watch a cloud form in this demonstration. Students hypothesize what will happen and complete a record sheet to record the results.

WEATHER • POCKET 2

Clouds

Cirrus clouds can be seen up high.

WEATHER • POCKET 2

Name:

Which Cloud Is It?

Draw lines to match each cloud with its name and the type of weather it can bring.

cumulus

stratus

cirrus

Draw the clouds you see today. Write their names

WEATHER • POCKET 3

Name:

A Cloud in a Jar

What we did:

What we saw:

What we learned:

POCKET 3

Thermometers **pages 51 and 52**

After discussing thermometers and seeing how they work, students will make a paper thermometer to use to make predictions before taking daily outside temperatures.

Recording the Temperature **page 53**

Record the outside temperature for a school week. Compare your class readings with the temperatures given in the local newspaper.

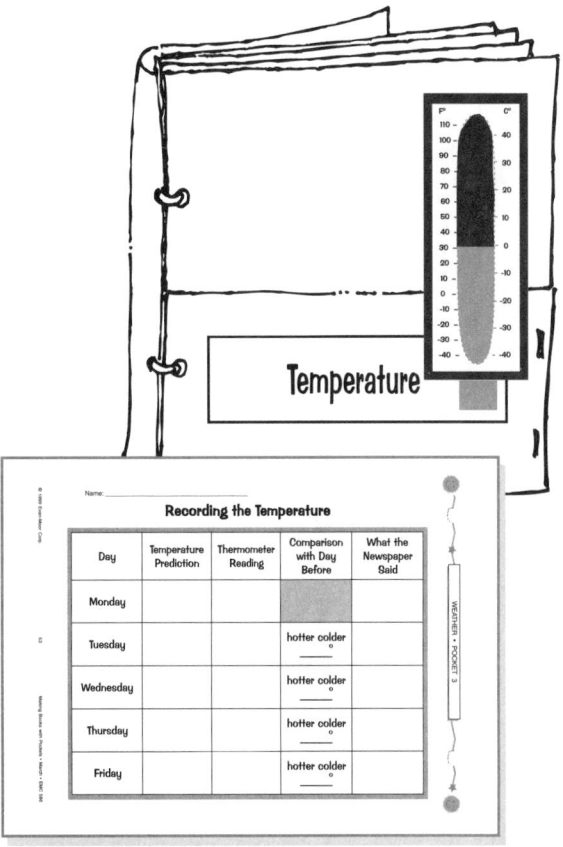

POCKET 4

Big Winds **pages 54 and 55**

After reading books about tornadoes and hurricanes, important facts are recorded on a chart and on individual record sheets.

3-D Tornado **page 56**

This "do-it-together" project results in a display of the weather elements that are found during tornado-producing conditions.

Note: Reproduce this cover decoration for students to color, cut out, and glue to the cover of their Weather books.

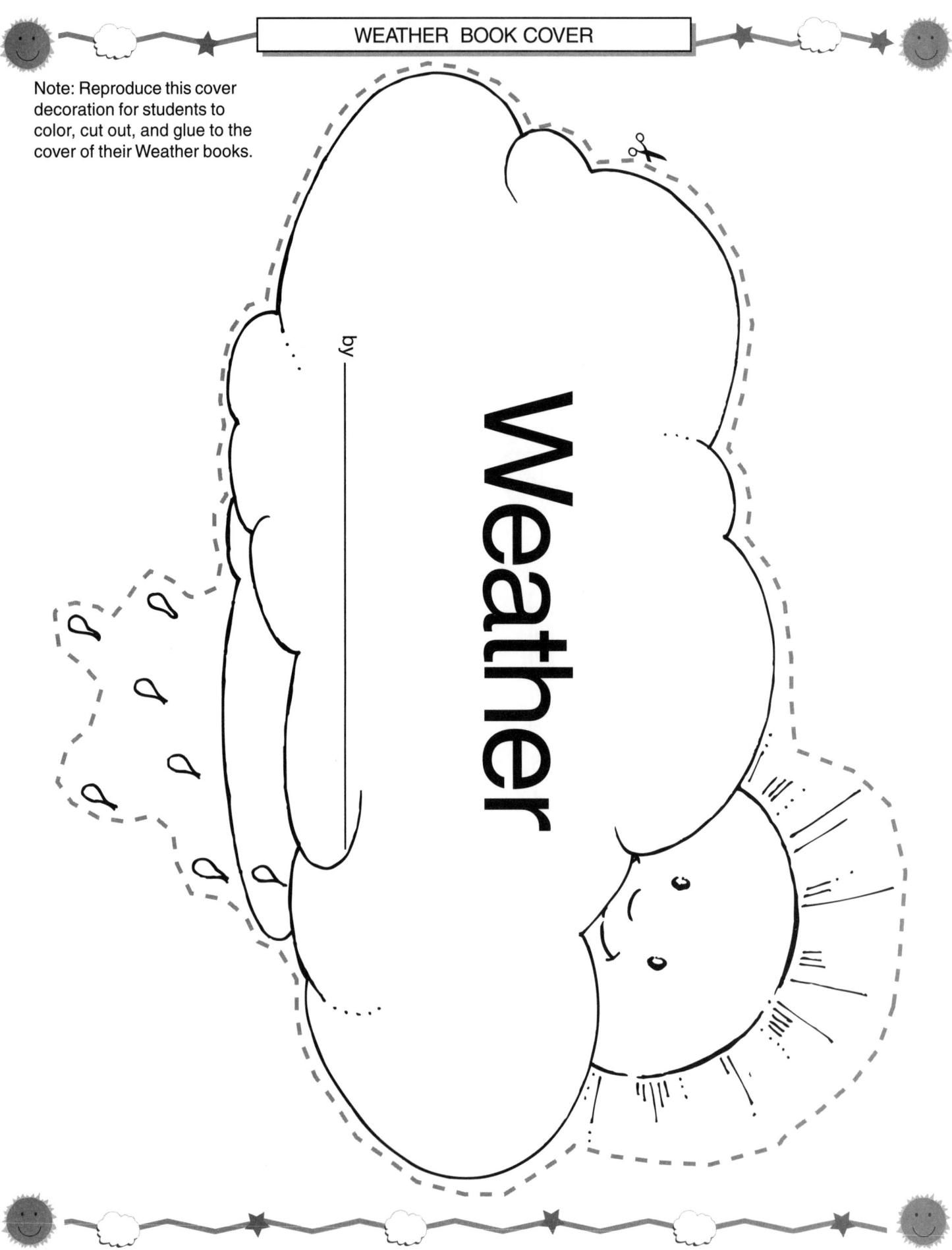

Weather

by _____

Water Cycle Book

Materials

- water cycle minibook on pages 42–45
- pencils
- crayons
- stapler

Steps to Follow

1. Read books that explain the water cycle. Some choices are:

    - *Water Dance* by Tomas Locker; Harcourt Brace & Co., 1997.

    - *A Drop of Water* by Walter Wick; Scholastic, 1997.

    - *Once Upon Ice* by Jane Yolen; Wordson/Boyds Mills Press, 1997.

2. Give students the pages of the water cycle book. Discuss each phase of the water cycle and confirm student understanding. As you discuss the cycle, write important terms on the chalkboard so that students may use them in their writing—vapor, evaporation, condensation, precipitation.

3. Students write the corresponding sentences for each step.

    (1) Precipitation—rain falls from the sky.

    (2) Rainwater collects in puddles, lakes, rivers, and oceans.

    (3) The warm sun heats the water, causing it to evaporate as water vapor.

    (4) The water vapor rises in the air and collects to form clouds in the sky.

    (5) If enough water collects in a cloud, the cloud appears dark.

    (6) When the cloud can no longer hold any more water vapor, it condenses to liquid water and rain occurs.

    (7) This process repeats and is called the water cycle.

4. Staple pages in order to complete the book.

Variation: The water cycle steps can also be glued in a circle on one large paper with arrows drawn between each step.

The
Water
Cycle

Name: _____

Making Books with Pockets • March • EMC 586

Making Books with Pockets • March • EMC 586

Making Books with Pockets • March • EMC 586

Making Books with Pockets • March • EMC 586

Making Books with Pockets • March • EMC 586

Making Books with Pockets • March • EMC 586

6

7

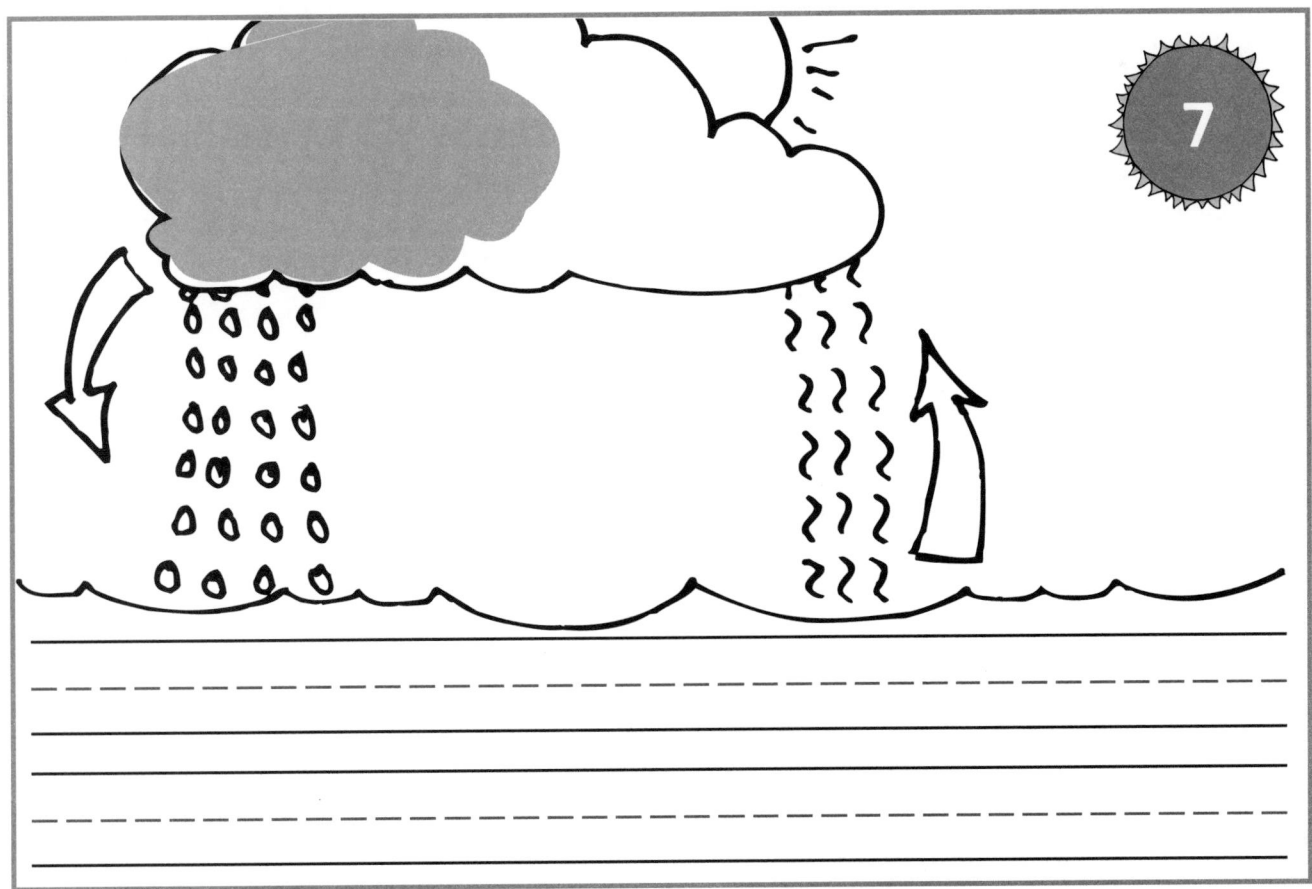

Types of Clouds

Materials

- a book on clouds (for example, *The Cloud Book* by Tomie de Paola)
- cloud poems on page 47 (make an overhead transparency and also reproduce the page for each student)
- worksheet on page 48
- pencils

Steps to Follow

1. Read as much of the book as is appropriate to the level of your group.

2. Discuss the three main types of clouds—cirrus, cumulus, and stratus.

3. Present the cloud poems on the overhead. Talk about the important characteristics of each type and note these in the illustrations. Give students copies of the poems for their "Types of Clouds" pockets.

4. Depending on the level of your students, do the worksheet together or independently.

Clouds

Cirrus clouds can be seen up high.

They drift and float through the beautiful sky.

Sheer, cold, and white against the blue,

Looking like mare's tails as the sun shines through.

Stratus clouds are low and gray.

There's a message they come to say,

Get out your umbrella, don't you know

I'm here to bring you rain or snow.

Cumulus clouds form pictures so great.

On a nice, sunny day you can watch them change shape.

But that's not all cumulus clouds do—

Thunderstorms and tornadoes come from them, too.

Name:

_____

Which Cloud Is It?

Draw lines to match each cloud with its
name and the type of weather it can bring.

cumulus

stratus

cirrus

Draw the clouds you see today. Write the name.

A Cloud in a Jar

Do this demonstration to help students understand that clouds are formed when water vapor cools and condenses.

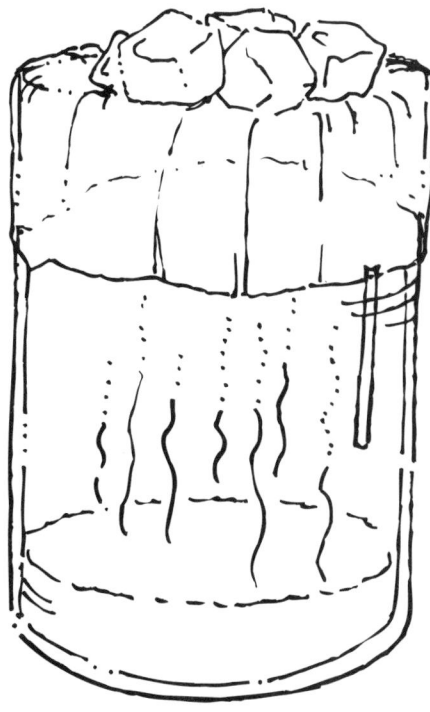

Materials

- jar
- plastic wrap
- ice
- water
- small pan
- tongs or oven mitt
- heat source
- record sheet on page 50

Step to Follow

1. Fill the jar with boiling water.

2. Pour out all but 1" (2.5 cm) of the water.

3. Cover the jar with the plastic wrap.

4. Place ice on the plastic wrap.

5. Students observe for several minutes. (The inside of the jar will cloud up.)

Follow Up

- Ask, "What did you see happen after the ice was put on top of the jar?"
  (It became foggy inside.)
  "Where did the water come from?"
  (It condensed from the water vapor in the air inside the jar.)
  "How is what happened like the way a cloud forms?"
  (Clouds are made up of millions of tiny drops formed when water vapor condenses.)

- Complete the record sheet individually or as a class, depending on the capabilities of your group.

Name: _____

A Cloud in a Jar

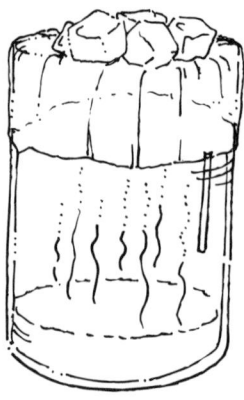

What we did:

_____
_ _
_____
_ _
_____
_ _
_____

What we saw:

_____
_ _
_____
_ _
_____
_ _
_____

What we learned:

_____
_ _
_____
_ _
_____
_ _
_____

Thermometers

Before constructing paper thermometers, make sure that students are familiar with thermometers and their functions.

- Show a thermometer. Ask students to name it and tell what it is used for. Talk about places where they have seen thermometers. Are there thermometers at school? Where? Do students have thermometers at home? How are they used?
- Make a list of the uses for thermometers that students come up with.
  - To tell the outside temperature.
  - To tell how warm it is in the house.
  - To tell if the oven is the right temperature to cook something.
- Ask how to tell the temperature on a thermometer. Guide students to express the idea that the higher (warmer) the temperature, the longer the column of red liquid (mercury) is.
- Place a thermometer in a glass of ice cubes and another in a glass of hot water. Ask students to predict which thermometer will read a higher temperature.

Materials

- thermometer pattern on page 52, reproduced on white construction paper
- two 4" x 10" (10 x 25.5 cm) pieces of black construction paper
- 2" x 12" (5 x 30.5 cm) red construction paper
- 2" x 12" (5 x 30.5 cm) tagboard
- scissors
- glue

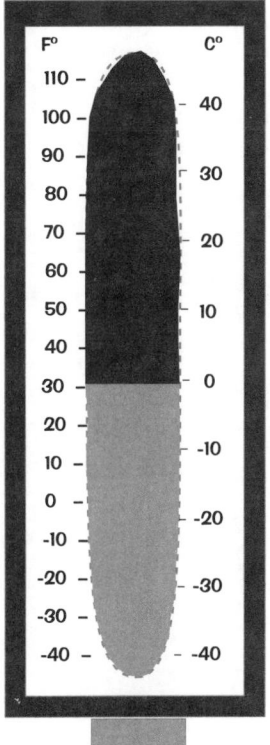

Steps to Follow

1. Cut out the thermometer and glue it to one piece of black paper.

2. Cut out the center of the white thermometer, cutting through the black paper as well.

3. Place glue along the top and side edges of the other piece of black construction paper. Lay the cut thermometer on top and press the edges.

4. Glue the red construction paper to the tagboard. Slip this inside to make the column of "mercury." Make sure the mercury can move up and down.

Use the thermometers to make temperature predictions before taking the daily outside temperature.

Thermometer Pattern

Fº	Cº		Fº	Cº
110 –			110 –	
100 –	– 40		100 –	– 40
90 –			90 –	
80 –	– 30		80 –	– 30
70 –	– 20		70 –	– 20
60 –			60 –	
50 –	– 10		50 –	– 10
40 –			40 –	
30 –	– 0		30 –	– 0
20 –			20 –	
10 –	– ⁻10		10 –	– ⁻10
0 –			0 –	
⁻10 –	– ⁻20		⁻10 –	– ⁻20
⁻20 –	– ⁻30		⁻20 –	– ⁻30
⁻30 –			⁻30 –	
⁻40 –	– ⁻40		⁻40 –	– ⁻40

Name: _____

Recording the Temperature

Day	Temperature Prediction	Thermometer Reading	Comparison with Day Before	What the Newspaper Said
Monday				
Tuesday			hotter colder ___°	
Wednesday			hotter colder ___°	
Thursday			hotter colder ___°	
Friday			hotter colder ___°	

Big Winds

Learning about Tornadoes and Hurricanes

Materials

- books about tornadoes and hurricanes (see bibliography on page 37)
- large chart paper
- marking pen
- "Big Winds" record sheet on page 55

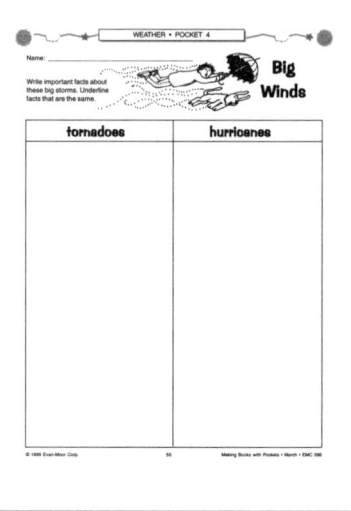

Steps to Follow

1. On the chart paper, draw an organizer similar to the "Big Winds" record sheet.

2. Read about tornadoes. (Pause during reading and ask students to tell information they have learned. Reread sections if necessary to help students recognize and understand important ideas.)

3. Record student ideas on the large chart.

4. If appropriate for your group, have students copy the information on their record sheet. (You may want to have them write only a few facts.)

5. Conduct a second lesson at another time to find out about hurricanes.

6. Underline any facts that are the same for the two storms.

Tornadoes

- Form from thunderstorms over land
- Cold air meets warm air and begins to spin
- Can be one mile across
- Found in U.S. only—Midwest and Florida
- Happen mostly in April, May, and June
- Winds can reach 300 mph (480 kph)
- Can't really tell where they will hit
- Cause a lot of damage

Hurricanes

- Form from thunderstorms over warm water
- Can be 200 miles across
- Found in Caribbean Sea, Gulf of Mexico, Indian Ocean, South China Sea, Timor Sea
- Happen mostly in August, September, and October
- Winds usually around 100 mph (160 kph)
- Lots of rain and big waves
- Can be predicted
- Cause a lot of damage

Name: _____

Write important facts about
these big storms. Underline
facts that are the same.

Big Winds

tornadoes	hurricanes

3-D Tornado

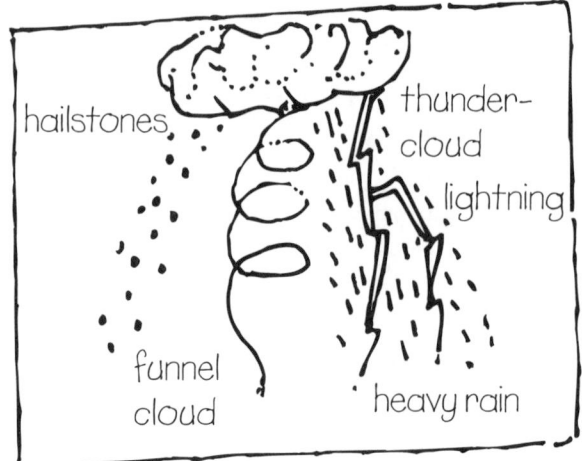

hailstones

thunder-cloud

lightning

funnel cloud

heavy rain

Materials

- 8" (20 cm) square gray, black, or dark blue tissue paper
- 18" (45.5 cm) piece of heavy string or yarn
- 9" x 12" (23 x 30.5 cm) light blue construction paper
- crayons
- glue

Introducing the Lesson

1. Read *Flash, Crash, Rumble, and Roll* by Franklyn M. Branley and review the information from the previous lesson about how tornadoes form.

2. List the various characteristics of a thunderstorm over land (tornado)—lightning, thundercloud, hail, rain, funnel cloud.

3. Have students follow step by step as you create a model illustrating the elements of a thunderstorm over land resulting in a tornado.

Steps to Follow

1. Form (scrunch) tissue paper into a cloud shape. Glue cloud to the top center of the light blue paper.

2. Glue string spiraling down from the center of the cloud.

3. Using crayons, color heavy rain and lightning bolts on one side of the string tornado.

4. On the other side use a white crayon to color hailstones.

5. Label the different characteristics of the storm: thundercloud, lightning, heavy rain, hailstones, and funnel cloud.

Note: Reproduce this page to label each of the four pockets of the Weather book.

Pocket 1

Water Cycle

Pocket 2

Types of Clouds

Pocket 3

Temperature

Pocket 4

Big Winds

Color a rainbow.

sun
sunny

clouds
cloudy

condensation

evaporation

precipitation
rain
rainy

wind
windy

water

lightning

tornado

hurricane

Making Books with Pockets • March • EMC 586

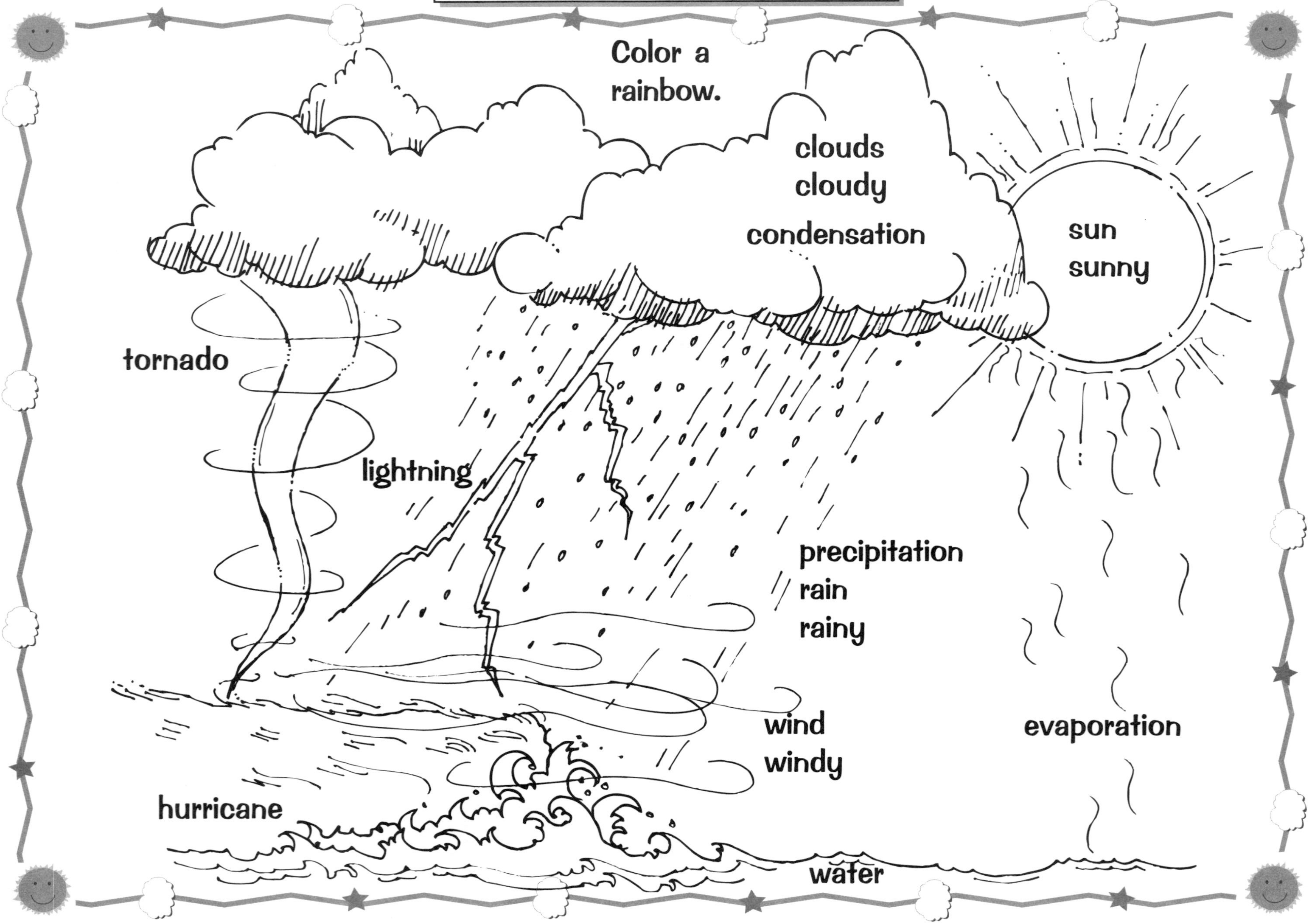

© 1999 Evan-Moor Corp.

Name: _____

Our Community

Learning about the community in which they live gives young students a sense of belonging to a place. In this pocket book, art, reading, and written and oral language activities provide opportunities to learn about people, places, and safety in the community.

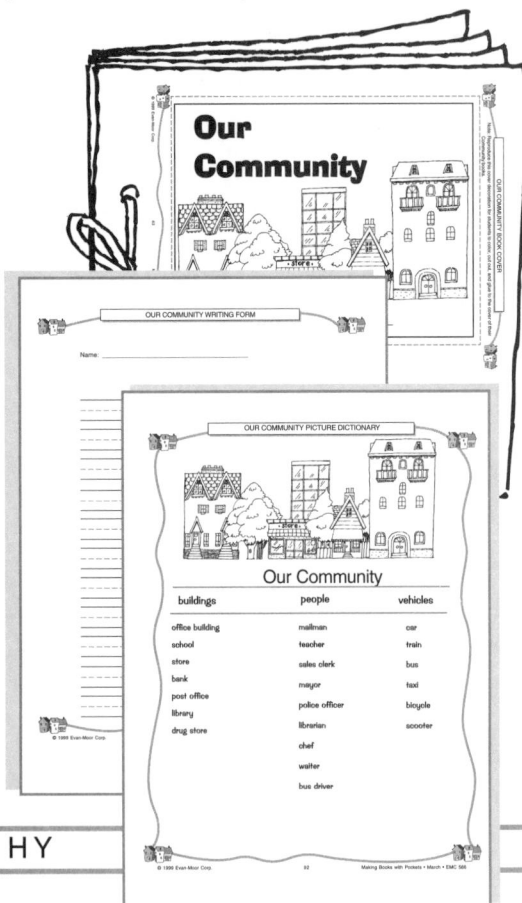

BIBLIOGRAPHY

A Day in the Life of a Police Officer by Eric Arnold; Scholastic, 1994.
Fire Fighter by Robert Maass; Scholastic, 1989.
I'm a Fire Fighter by Mary Packard; Scholastic, 1995.
Look Around the City by Patricia Malfatti; Grosset & Dunlap, 1993.
Taxi: A Book of City Words by Betsy & Guilio Maestro; Clarion Books, 1989.
Walter the Baker by Eric Carle; Scholastic, 1995.

Other Evan-Moor resource materials on the community include:
PreK–1:
    My Neighborhood (EMC 546)
    Helping Hands (EMC 547)
Grades 1–3:
    My Community (EMC 552)
    Around My Town (EMC 4141)

Community Helpers   pages 64–70

Learn about those whose jobs make our communities run, and make community helper figures from patterns provided.

Comparing Two Important Jobs— Fire Fighter/Police Officer   pages 71–73

Read and talk about the aspects of these vital community jobs. Compare the roles by making a Venn diagram adorned by hats of the two professions.

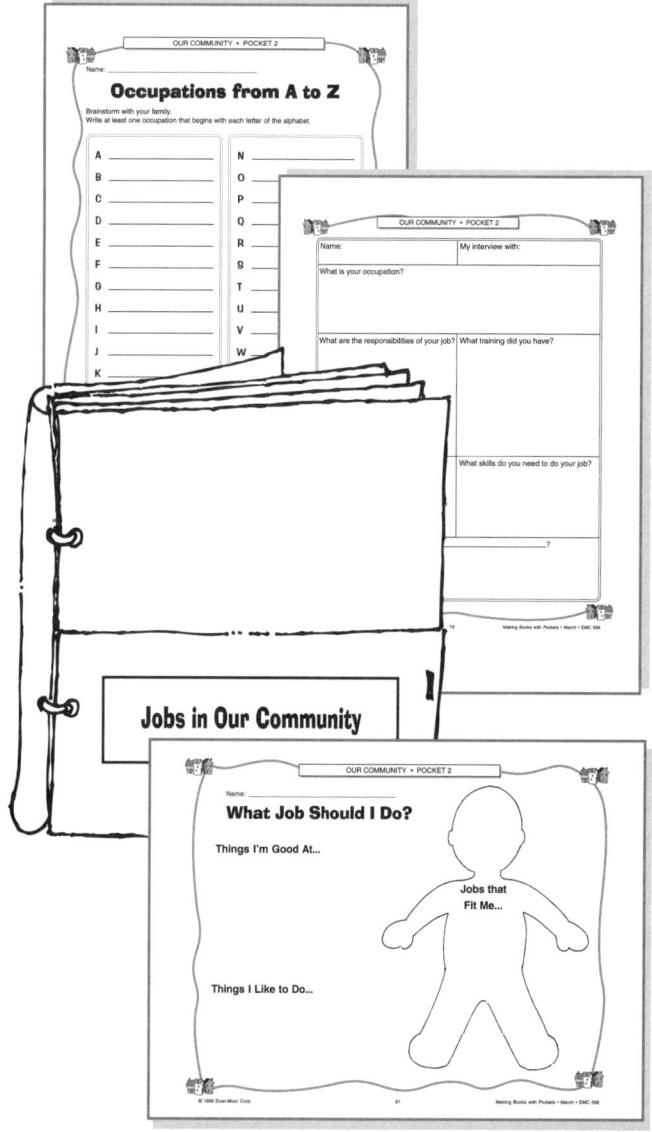

The ABCs of Occupations   pages 74–76

Each student does a page for the class occupations book and makes a copy for his or her "Jobs in Our Community" pocket.

Interview a Community Worker   pages 77–79

As a homework assignment with adult assistance, students will interview a community worker and complete an interview form.

What Job Should I Do?   pages 80 and 81

Students think about what they are good at and what they like to do and record what types of jobs they might consider.

POCKET 3

Places in Our Community   **page 82**

Students locate and record businesses
and other community buildings
on a homework form.

A Fold-Out Community   **pages 83–86**

Create a colorful depiction of
important places in your community
with this cut-paper, fold-out project.

POCKET 4

My Safety Book   **pages 87–89**

Students read and complete a minibook
to illustrate ways that they stay safe.

**Do You Know
Safety Signs?**   **Page 90**

Discuss how signs can help to keep us safe.
Have children describe signs they see in the
community. Complete the worksheet to show
recognition of some important safety signs.

Note: Reproduce this cover decoration for students to color, cut out, and glue to the cover of their Community books.

Our Community

by _____

Community Helpers

Read a number of books on community helpers. See the bibliography on page 60 and add others from your library. (Troll Associates has a series called *What's It Like to Be a...?* that describes the jobs of various community workers such as a postal worker, teacher, veterinarian, etc.)

A basic body pattern and clothing patterns for five community workers are provided. You may want students to make several or all of these figures for their pocket books. Encourage students to use the basic body pattern and design additional community helpers.

Add short written descriptions of each worker to the pocket. These may be written on the back of the figures or on a paper "tag" that you attach to the worker's hand.

Materials

- body pattern on page 65, reproduced on manila or brown paper
- clothing patterns on pages 66–70, reproduced on white construction paper
- crayons
- scissors
- glue

Steps to Follow

1. Cut out the basic body shape.

2. Color and cut out the clothing for the community helpers. Glue clothing onto the body.

3. Add facial features, hair, and other details with torn or cut paper and felt pens.

Extension

You may want to glue the figures to craft sticks to create puppets. Let students create short skits to show what they have learned about community helpers.

Basic Body Pattern

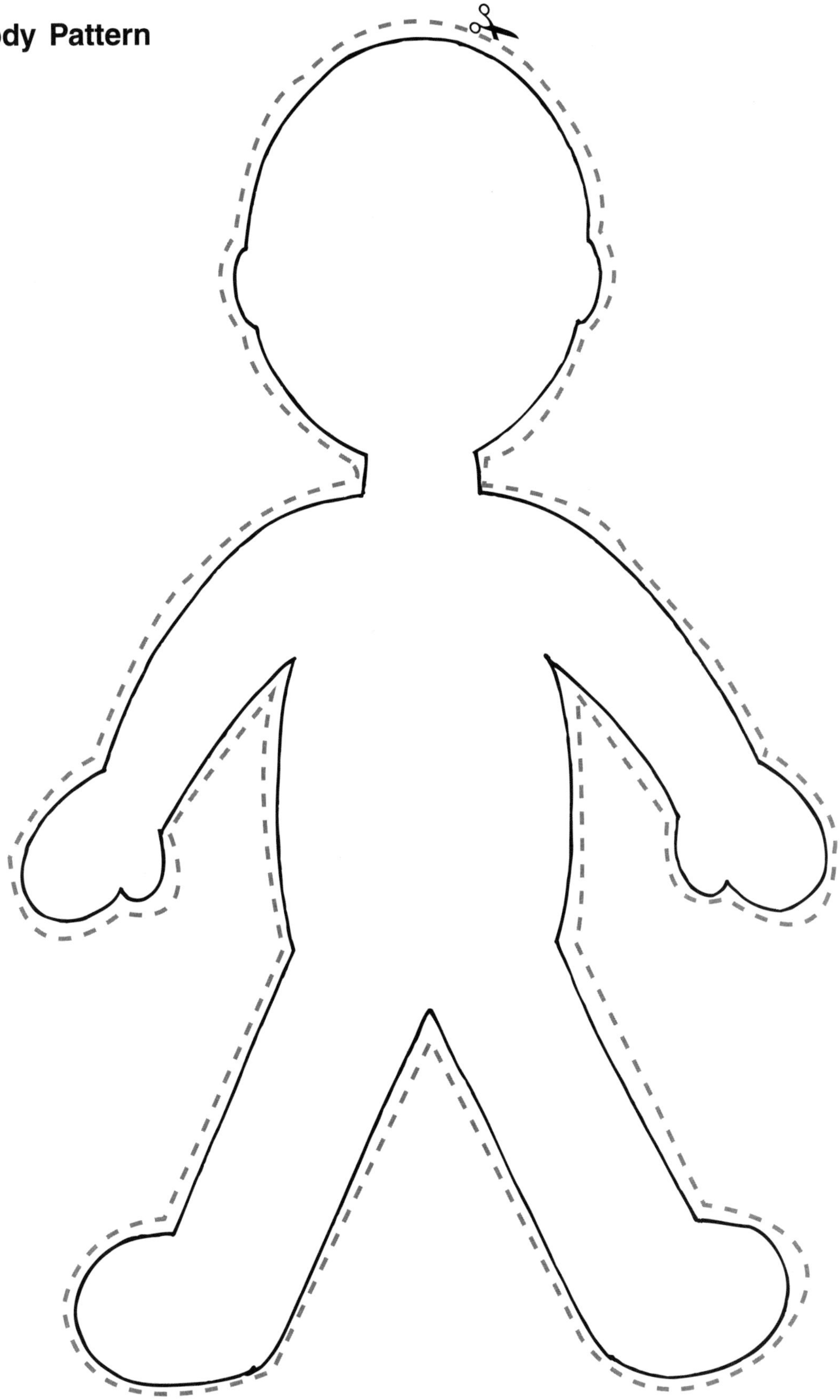

Chef

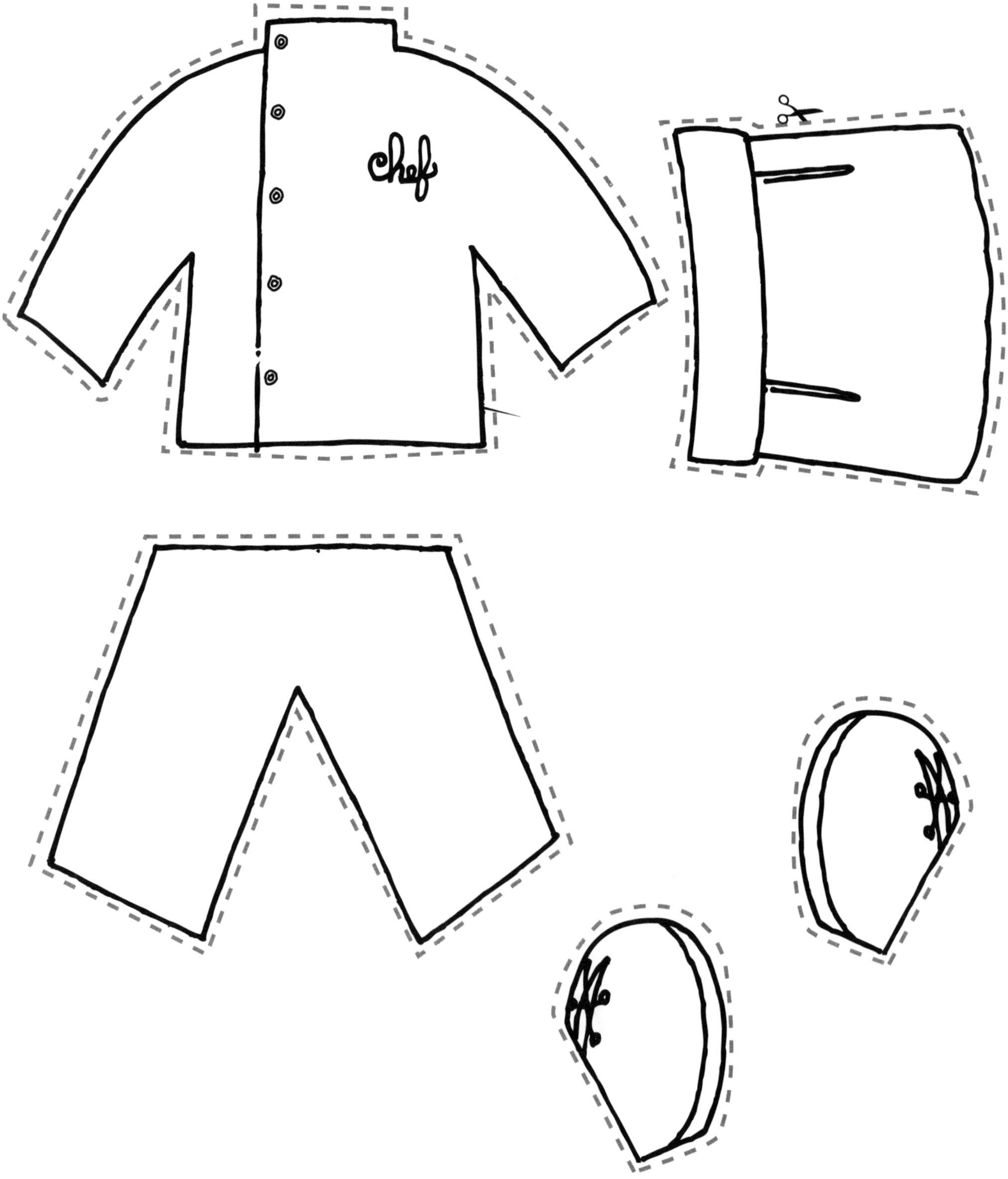

Chef

Librarian

The Three Little Pigs

The
Little
Red
Hen

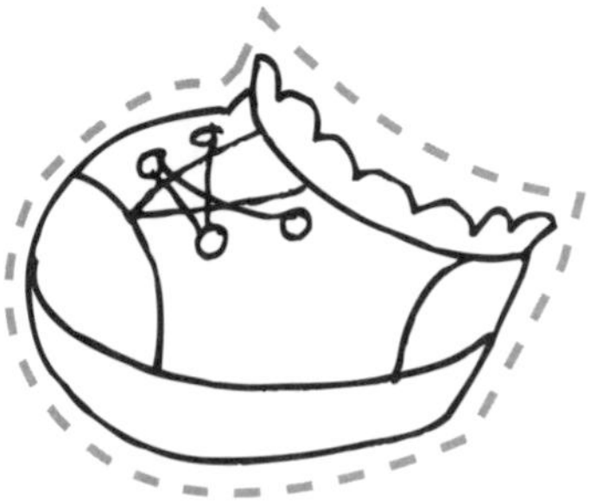

Fire Fighter

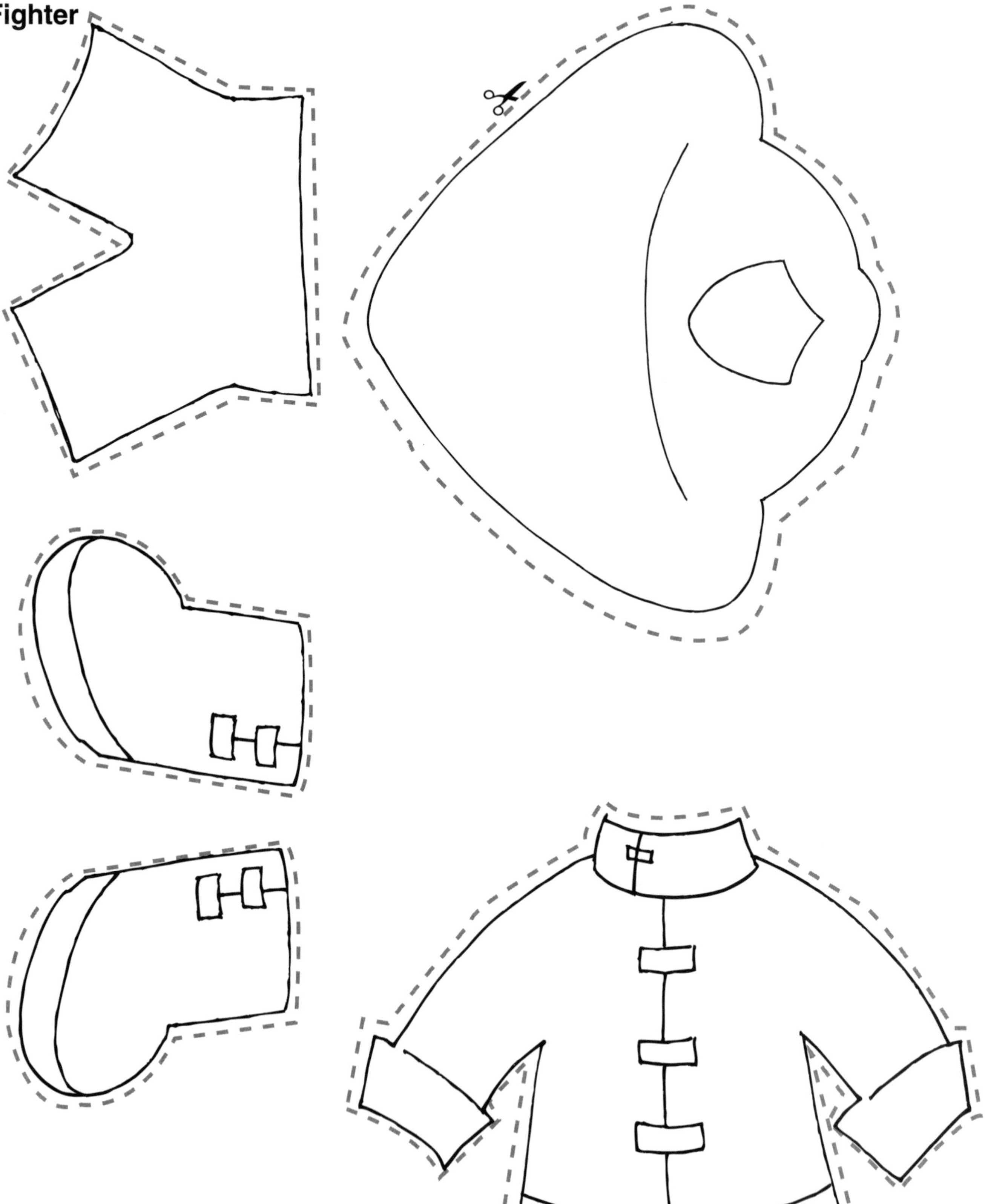

Doctor

Farmer

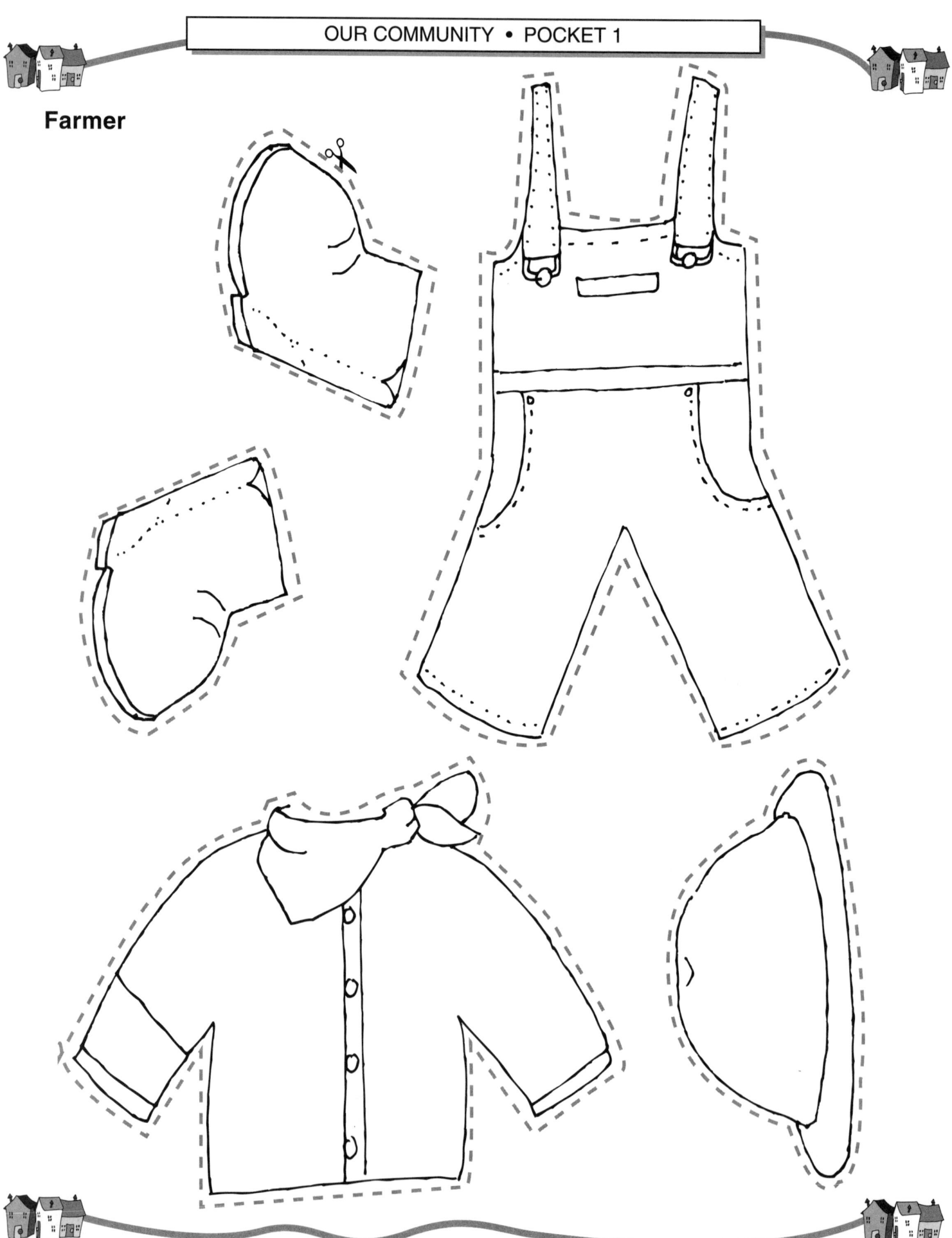

Comparing Two Important Jobs—
Fire Fighter and Police Officer

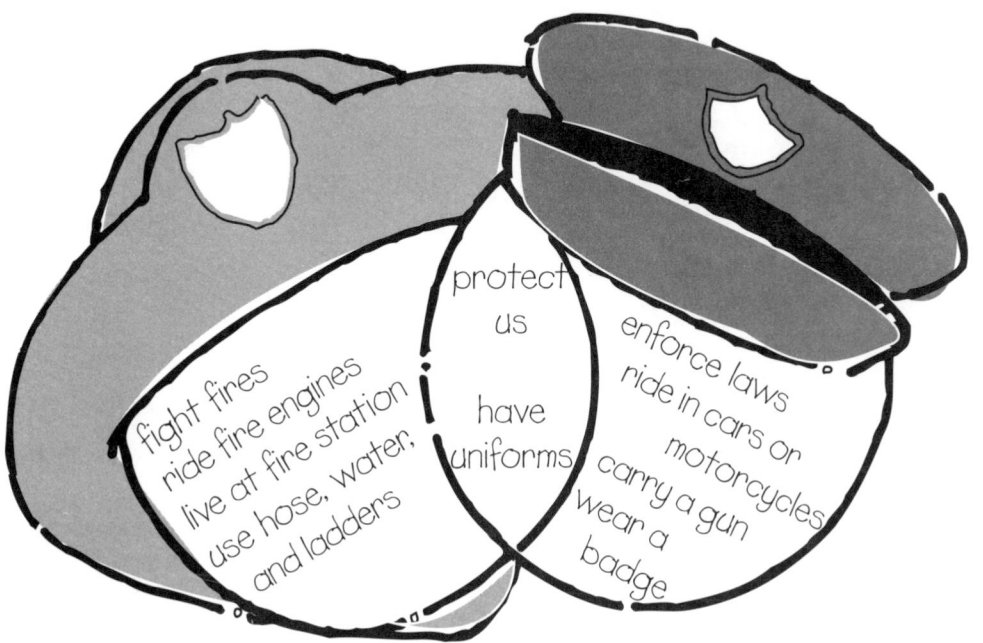

Materials

- Venn diagram on page 72, reproduced on white construction paper
- hat patterns on page 73, reproduced on white construction paper
- crayons
- scissors
- glue

Steps to Follow

1. Read *A Day in the Life of a Police Officer* and *I'm a Fire Fighter* to your class.

2. Make a sample Venn diagram, large enough for your class to see, on a chart, chalkboard, or overhead projector.

3. Brainstorm ways that a fire fighter and a police officer are similar and different. Write the attributes in the appropriate part of the Venn diagram.

4. To finish the project, cut out the Venn diagram. Then color and cut out the two hats and glue them to the diagram.

5. Students copy the attributes on to their Venn diagrams.

Venn Diagram

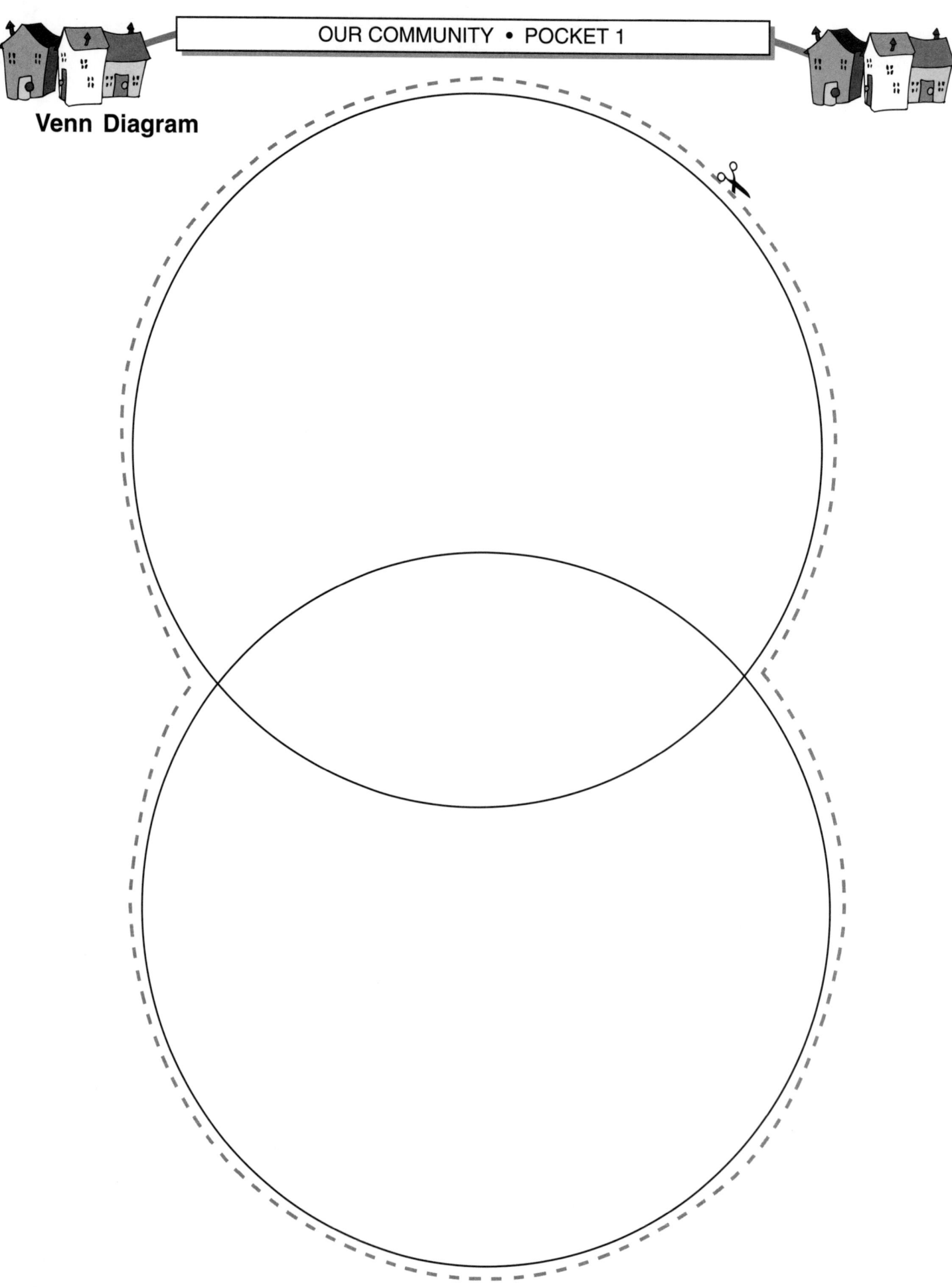

**Hats for
Venn Diagram**

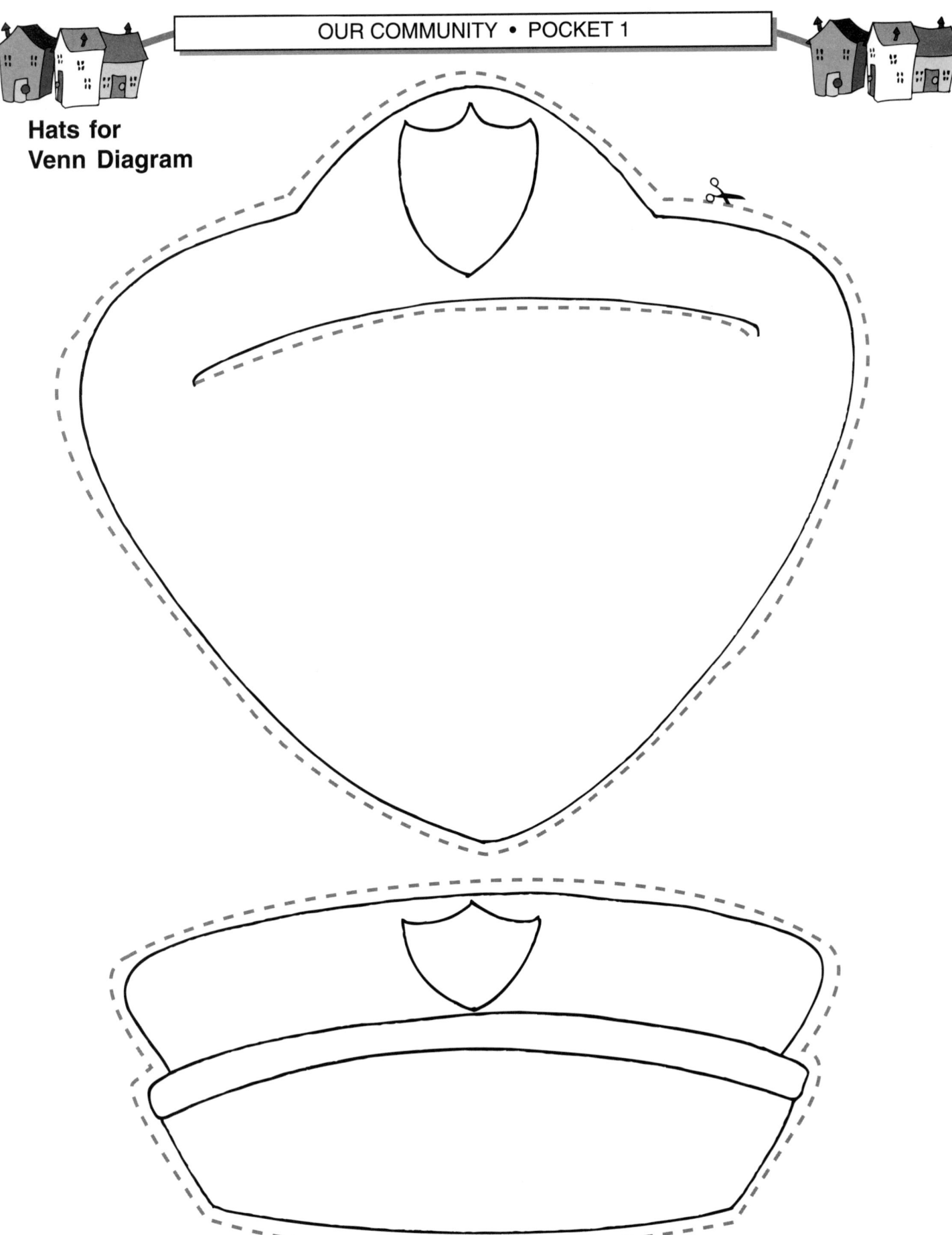

73

The ABCs of Occupations

Students compile a list of occupations from A to Z and then create a class book.

Materials

- research sheet on page 75
- form for class book on page 76, 2 per student

Steps to Follow

1. Students take home the form on page 75 and try to list an occupation for every letter of the alphabet. (Depending on the level of your class, you may want to make each student responsible for only certain letters.)

2. Share findings and compile a class list of occupations.

3. Assign each student a letter and provide two copies of page 76—one copy for the class book and one for the student's pocket book.

4. Each student writes the letter he or she has been given and the name of an occupation beginning with that letter. The student also writes and draws about that occupation. Each student then makes a copy of the page to place in the pocket of his or her "Our Community" book.

5. Assemble the book in alphabetical order. Add a front and back cover and display the book in your classroom library.

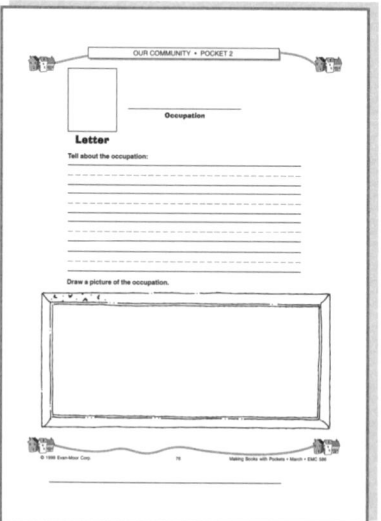

Name: _____

Occupations from A to Z

Brainstorm with your family.
Write at least one occupation that begins with each letter of the alphabet.

A _____

B _____

C _____

D _____

E _____

F _____

G _____

H _____

I _____

J _____

K _____

L _____

M _____

N _____

O _____

P _____

Q _____

R _____

S _____

T _____

U _____

V _____

W _____

X _____

Y _____

Z _____

_____

Occupation

Letter

Tell about the occupation:

_____

_____

_____

_____

_____

_____

_____

_____

_____

_____

Draw a picture of the occupation.

 Making Books with Pockets • March • EMC 586

Interview a Community Worker

After seeing an interview modeled and then practicing one in class, students will interview a family member, neighbor, or family friend to find out about that person's job.

Materials

- interview form on page 78
- cardboard clipboard with pencil
- parent letter on page 79

Steps to Follow

1. Discuss what an interview is. Have students seen someone being interviewed on television? What happens in an interview?

2. To model the interview process, ask a school staff member to come to the classroom to be interviewed by you. Describe what you are doing as you conduct the interview. ("I am going to introduce myself to Mr. Jones and tell him what I will be doing. I am going to write down what Mr. Jones said.")

3. As a class, interview another member of the school staff. Assign specific questions to individual students. Each student will ask his or her question in turn and be responsible for writing the answer.

4. Send home the interview form and the parent letter so that students can interview a worker of their choice.

5. When interview forms are returned, share a few each day.

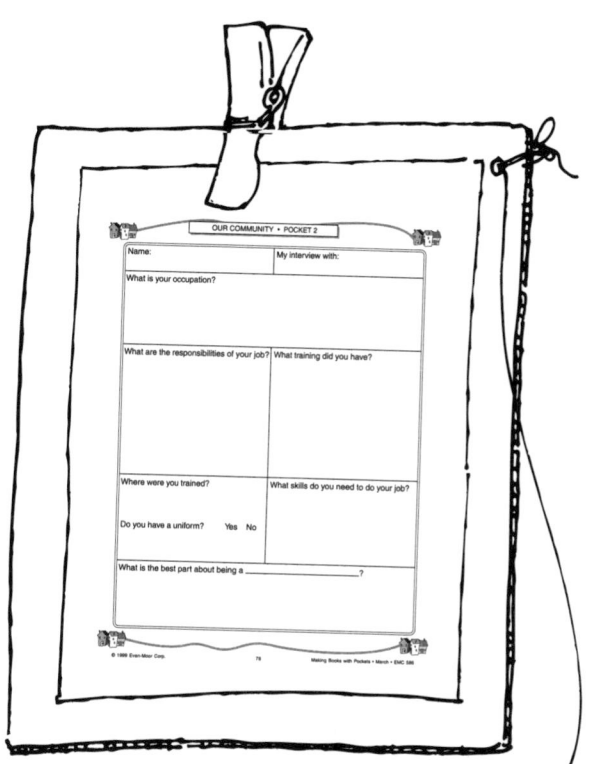

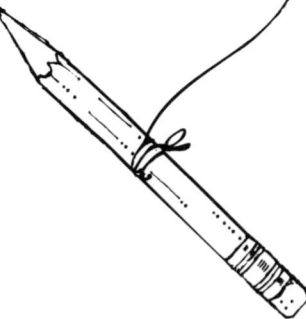

Name:

My interview with:

What is your occupation?

What are the responsibilities of your job?

What training did you have?

Where were you trained?

Do you have a uniform?   Yes   No

What skills do you need to do your job?

What is the best part about being a _____?

Dear Parent,

In our class, we have been talking about people who work in our community. We have interviewed some workers at school to practice our interview skills.

Please help your child conduct an interview with a family member, neighbor, or other adult to find out about that person's job.

You may want to have your child ask the questions while you record the person's responses. If you'd like, consider videotaping the interview.

Your child is to return the interview form to school by _____.

Thank you.

Dear Parent,

In our class, we have been talking about people who work in our community. We have interviewed some workers at school to practice our interview skills.

Please help your child conduct an interview with a family member, neighbor, or other adult to find out about that person's job.

You may want to have your child ask the questions while you record the person's responses. If you'd like, consider videotaping the interview.

Your child is to return the interview form to school by _____.

Thank you.

What Job Should I Do?

The purpose of this activity is to help students focus on their personal qualities when thinking of possible future careers.

You will need the writing form on page 81, reproduced for each student.

Presenting the Lesson

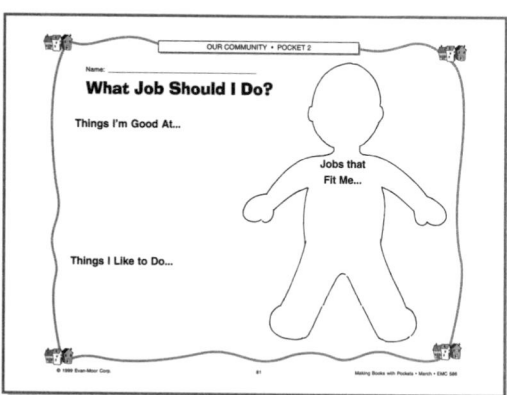

1. Things I'm Good at...
   As a whole group, brainstorm and list possible qualities for this section (storytelling, sports, painting, reading, math, cooking, drawing, writing, science, sewing, singing).

   Don't neglect qualities also (helping others, listening, being loyal, being kind, etc.).

   On their personal worksheets, students list those qualities that they feel apply to themselves.

2. Things I Like to Do...
   As a whole group, brainstorm and list possible activities. Some of these may be the same as mentioned above (swim, read cartoons, play with animals, give puppet shows, watch TV, build things, garden, talk to my friends, meet new people, help around the house).

   Encourage students to consider things they would like to learn also.

   On their personal worksheets, students list activities that apply to them.

3. Discuss various careers with students. Use the ABC list of occupations compiled on page 75 as a reference. Have students list several jobs that fit their personal qualities.

4. Students color the person on the form to look like themselves.

What Job Should I Do?

Name: _____

Things I'm Good at...

Jobs that Fit Me...

Things I Like to Do...

Making Books with Pockets • March • EMC 586

Name: _____

Places in Our Community

Find the names of places in your community.
Look carefully at each place.
Try to remember special features that each place has.

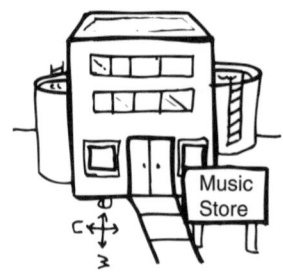

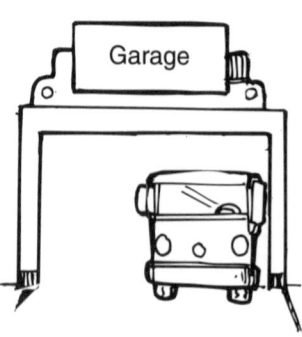

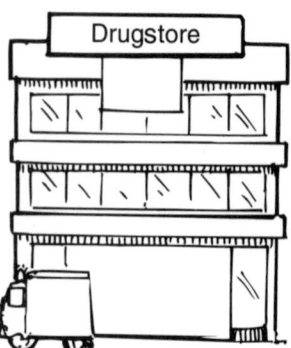

Making Books with Pockets • March • EMC 586

Fold-Out Community

Materials

- 6" x 36" (15 x 91.5 cm) white butcher paper
- scraps of assorted construction paper
- markers
- glue
- scissors

- roof patterns, reproduced from pages 84 and 85
- clip art patterns, reproduced from page 86

Presenting the Lesson

1. Brainstorm with your class and list the various buildings in your community using the "Places in Our Community" record forms previously completed. (Save this list to use in creating the 3-D community bulletin board described on page 96.)

2. Discuss what features and characteristics are special for each building. For example, fruit stands, mailboxes, flagpoles, steps, driveways, steeples, patios, carports, etc.

Steps to Follow

1. Accordian-fold butcher paper in fourths.

2. Glue a roof pattern to the top edge of each section.

3. Use scrap paper to create windows and doors.

4. Color and cut clip art and glue to the appropriate building.

5. Draw additional objects as desired.

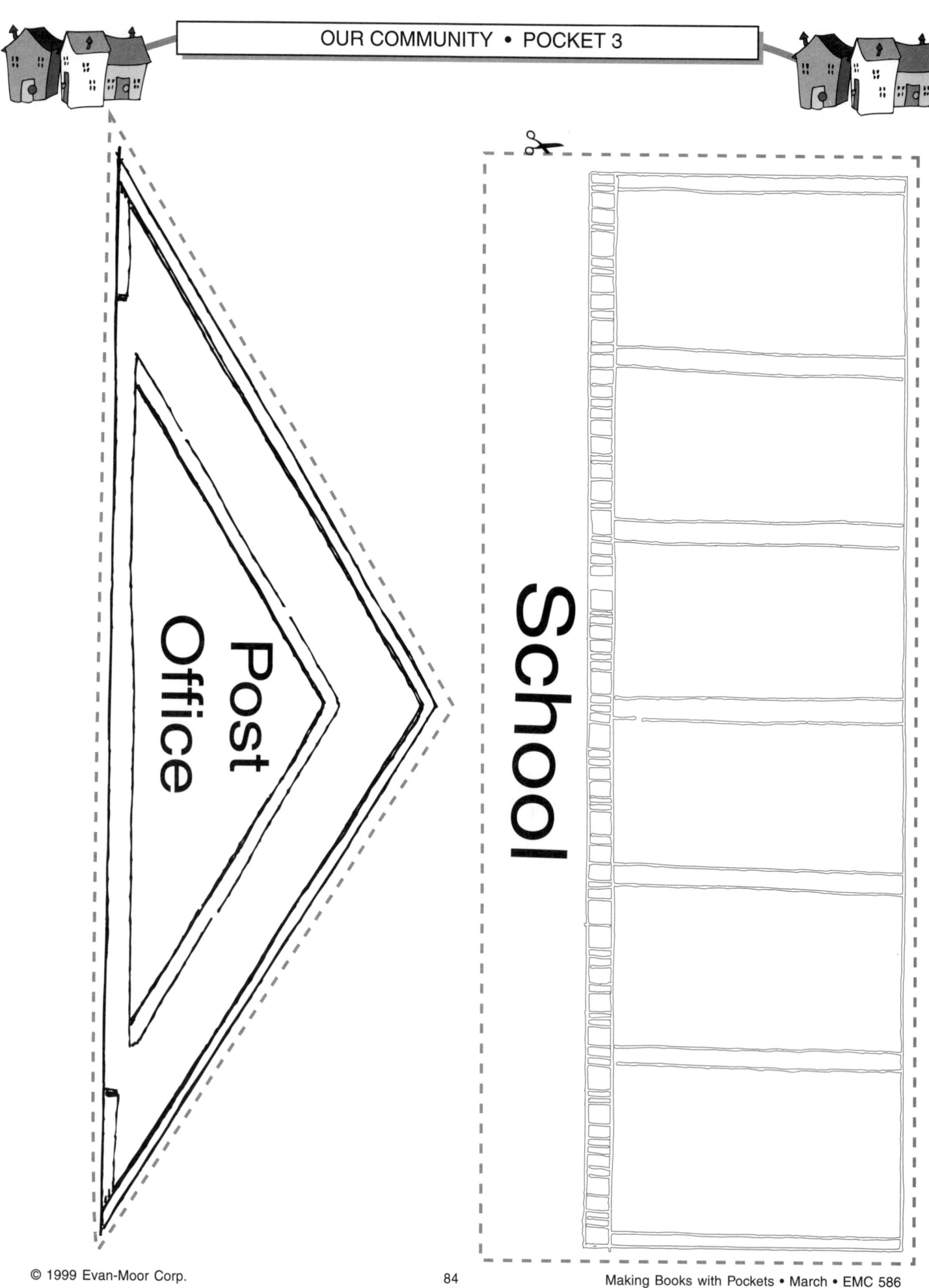

Post Office

School

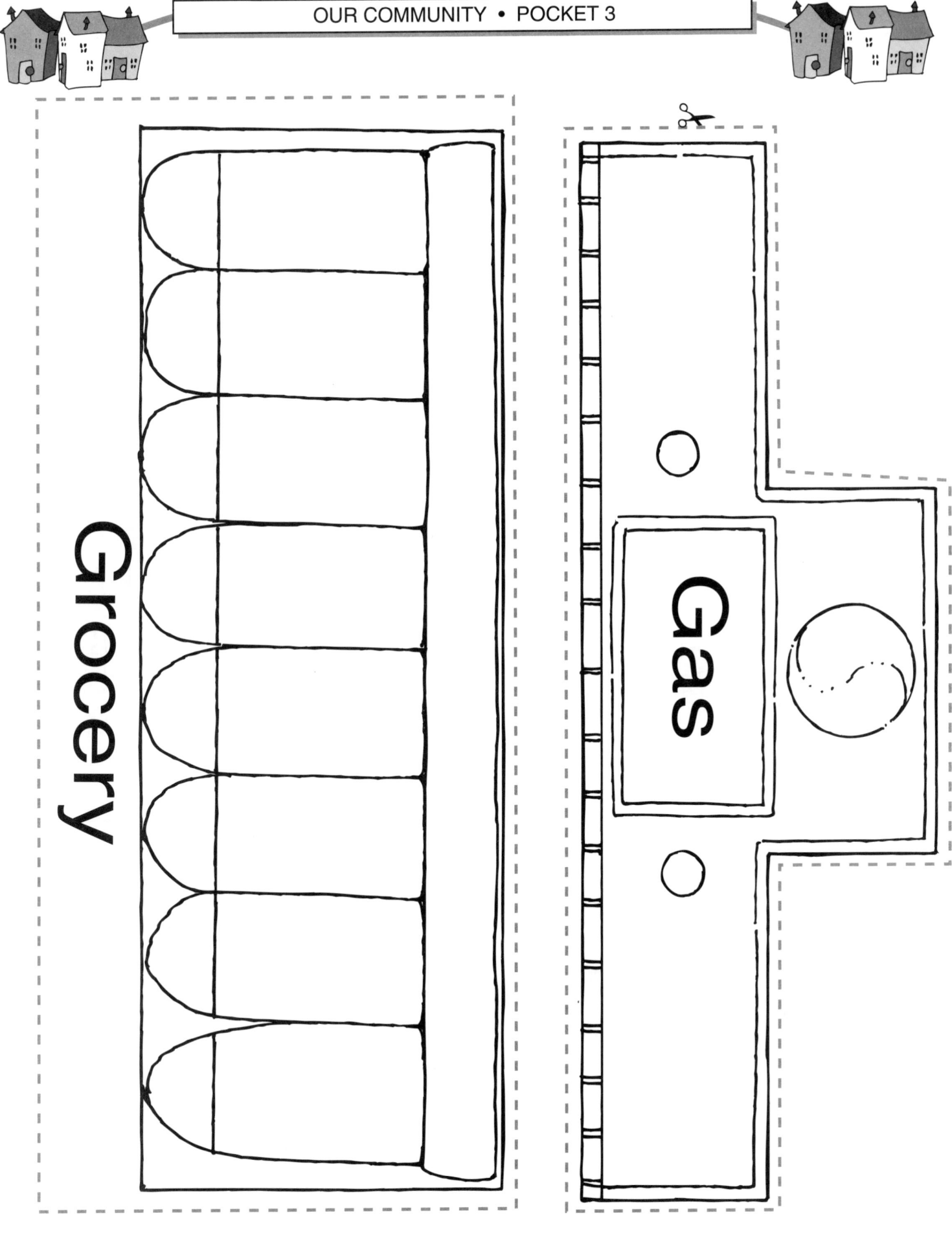

Grocery

Gas

Making Books with Pockets • March • EMC 586

Clip Art Patterns

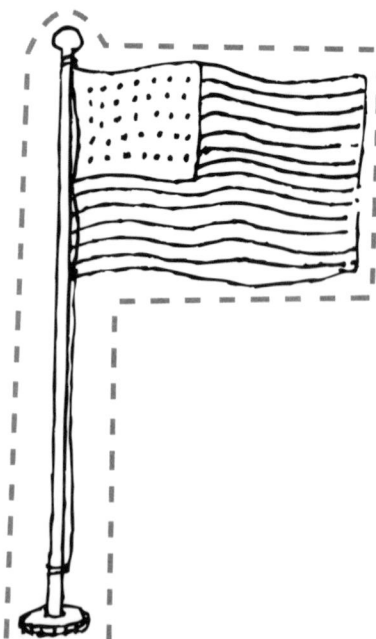

Mail

My Safety Book

by: _____

Making Books with Pockets • March • EMC 586

© 1999 Evan-Moor Corp.

When riding my bike, I stay safe...

_____

_____

Making Books with Pockets • March • EMC 586

© 1999 Evan-Moor Corp.

When I am at home, I stay safe...

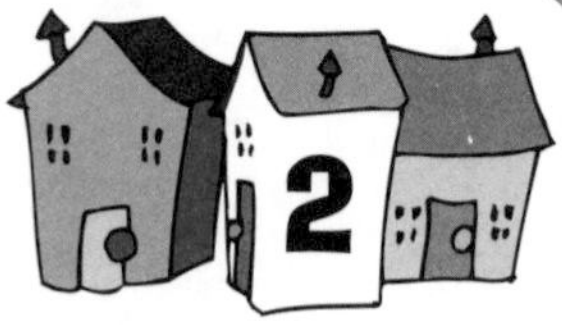

_____

_____

2

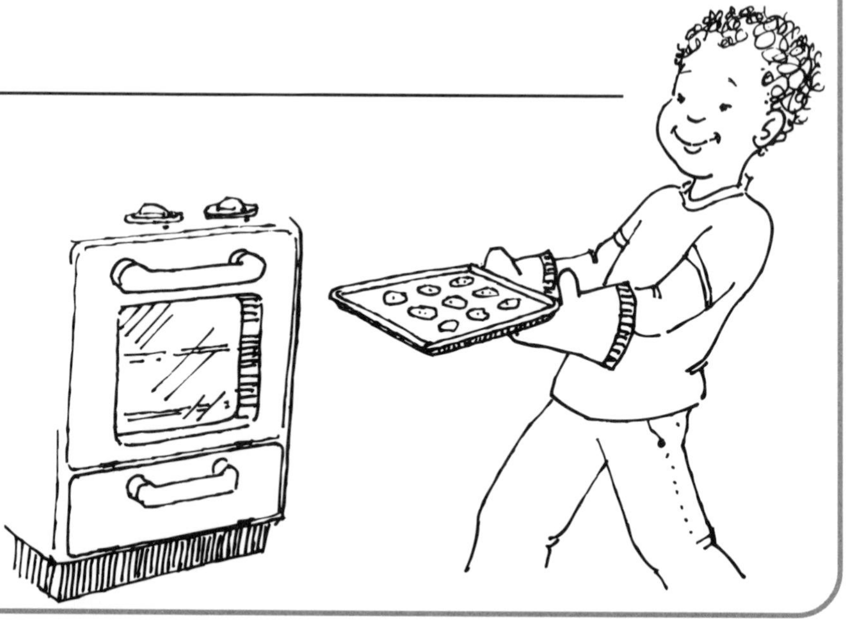

When I see a stranger, I stay safe...

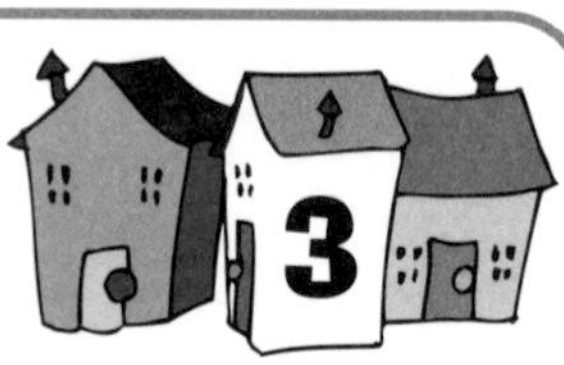

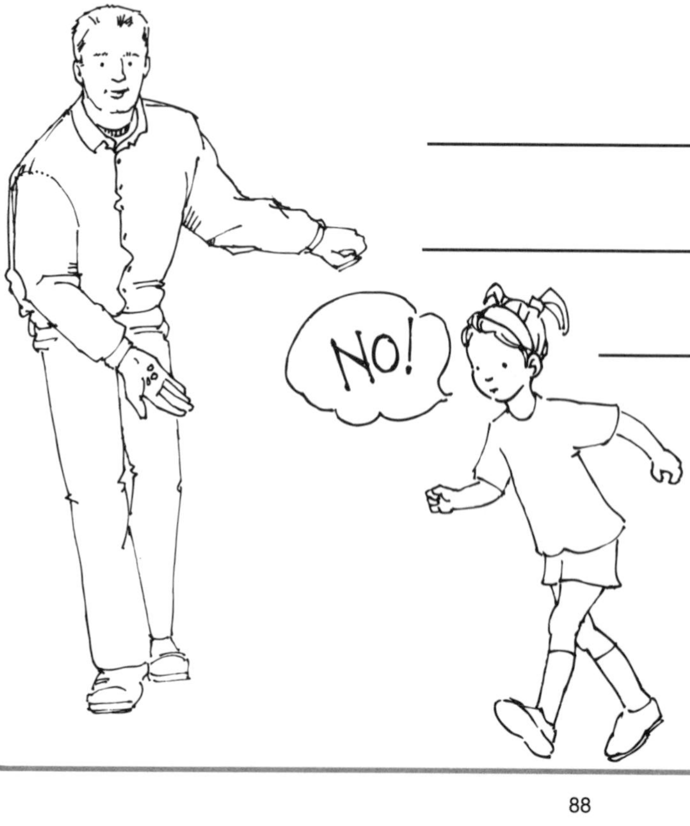

NO!

_____

_____

3

When crossing the street, I stay safe...

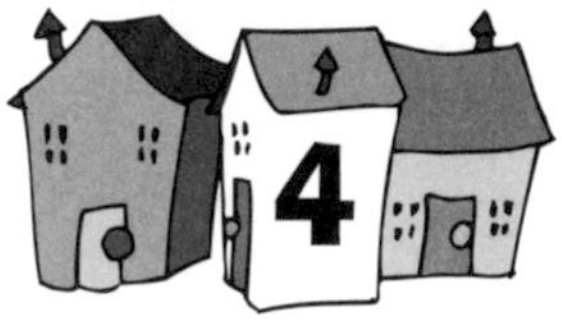

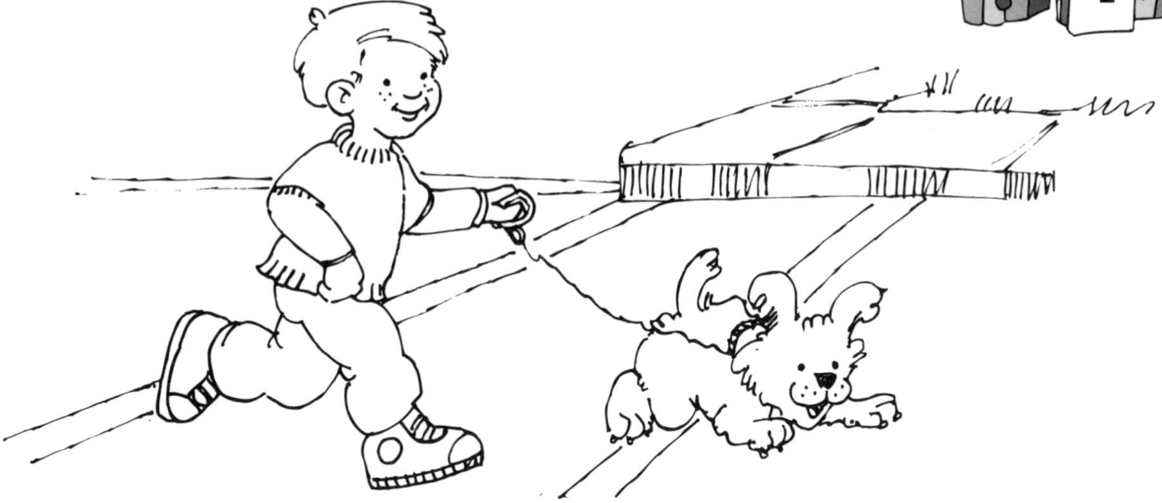

When riding in the car, I stay safe...

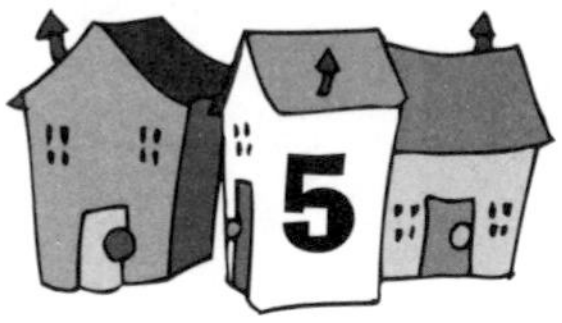

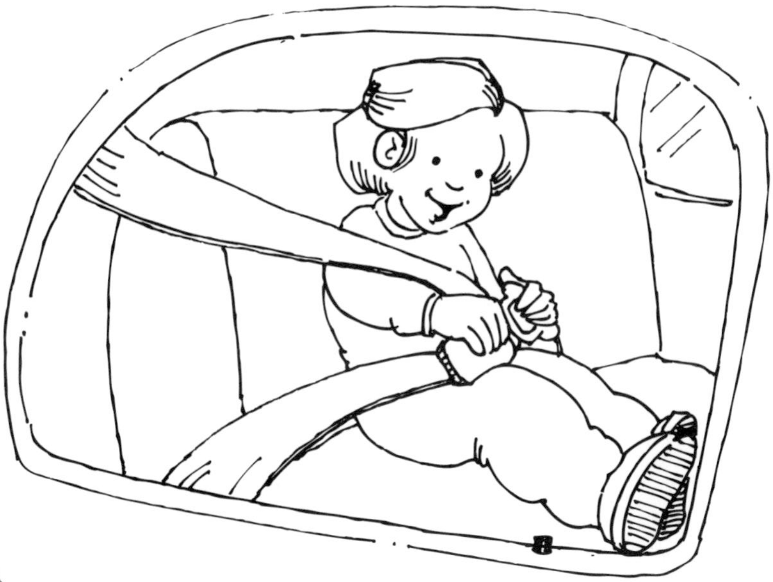

Name: _____

Do You Know Safety Signs?

Draw a line to match each sign with what it tells you.

I can cross the street here.

I can ride here.

I cannot ride here.

I must look for a train.

This could make me very sick.

I could slip and fall.

Making Books with Pockets • March • EMC 586

Note: Reproduce this page to label each of the four pockets of the Community book.

Pocket 1

Workers in Our Community

Pocket 2

Jobs in Our Community

Pocket 3

Places in Our Community

Pocket 4

Safety in Our Community

offices apartment

duplex shop

Our Community

buildings	people	vehicles
office building	mail carrier	car
school	teacher	train
store	sales clerk	bus
bank	mayor	taxi
post office	police officer	bicycle
library	librarian	scooter
drugstore	chef	
	waiter	
	bus driver	

  **OUR COMMUNITY WRITING FORM**

Name: _____

_____

_____

_____

_____

_____

_____

_____

_____

_____

_____

_____

_____

_____

_____

_____

_____

_____

_____

_____

_____

_____

93   *Making Books with Pockets* • March • EMC 586

Bulletin Board Bonanza

Plotting Temperatures Bulletin Board—page 95
Cooperative groups are each responsible for recording the daily temperature of a different U.S. city on a large wall graph.

Follow Up

Discuss information that can be learned from the graph. Ask questions such as:

"Which city had the highest and the lowest temperature this week?"

"How many degrees separated the highest and lowest temperatures?"

"What city had the biggest temperature change from one day to the next?"

3-D Community Bulletin Board—page 96
Cooperative groups design and make 3-D buildings from food boxes to complete a community bulletin board.

Follow Up

1. Use the completed bulletin board to practice map skills. Ask questions such as:

"In what direction would you walk to go from _____ to _____?"

"Can you give me directions to get from _____ to _____?"

2. Have each group write descriptions about their buildings and then post them around the bulletin board.

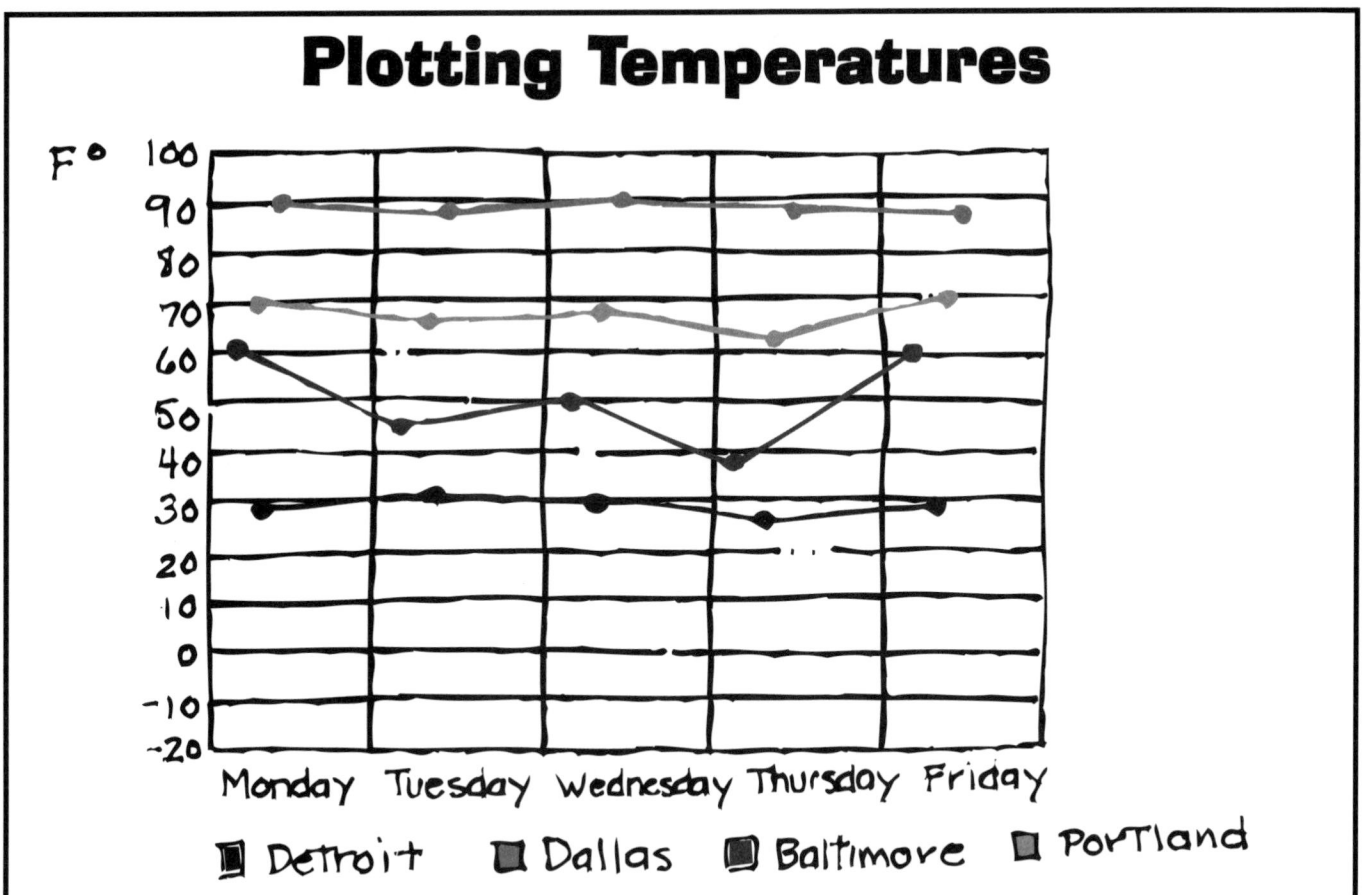

Materials

- white butcher paper
- wide black marking pen
- yard/meter stick
- four different colors of yarn or roving
- push pins
- weather section of a daily newspaper or an Internet weather site (e.g., go to www.cnn.com and select weather from the menu).

Divide the class into cooperative groups.

Explain the graph grid and locate the cities on a U.S. map. Assign a city to each group.

Every day each group will find the previous day's high temperature for its city and place a push pin on the graph to show that temperature.

After a week's temperatures are recorded, use yarn or roving to connect the push pins for each city.

Teacher Preparation

1. Cut butcher paper to fit a small bulletin board.

2. Choose cities in locations that are likely to offer variations in temperature (e.g., Detroit, MI; Dallas, TX; Baltimore, MD; Portland, OR). You will need as many cities as groups of students.

3. Draw a graph grid as shown above.

4. Staple the graph grid to the bulletin board.

3-D Community
A Bulletin Board

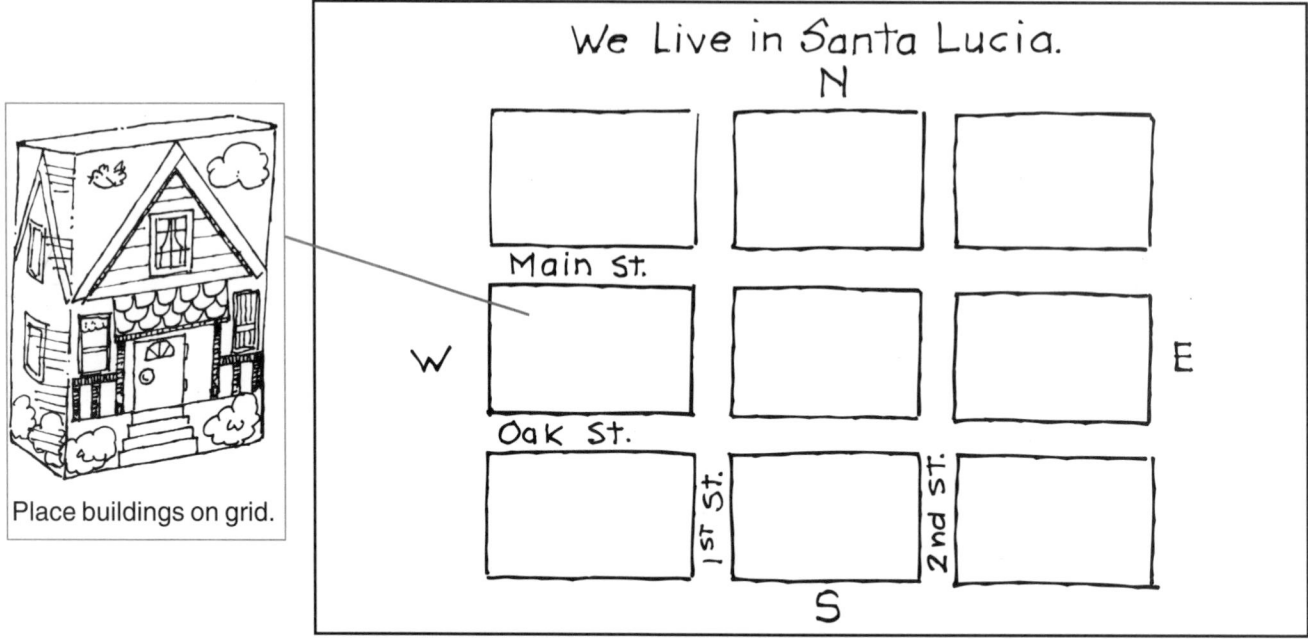

We Live in Santa Lucia.

N

Main St.

W

Oak St.

1st St.

2nd St.

E

S

Place buildings on grid.

Students work together in small groups to construct 3-D buildings to place on a bulletin board street grid.

Materials

- white butcher paper
- wide black marking pen
- paper food boxes in a variety of shapes and sizes (cereal, cake mixes, etc.)
- construction paper in a variety of colors and sizes, from full sheets to scraps
- glue
- scissors
- marking pens and/or crayons

Teacher Preparation

1. Cut the butcher paper to fit a large board.

2. Sketch city blocks, streets, and boulevards similar to the example shown. Add any features that are integral parts of your community—a lake, a large central park or town square, etc.

3. Outline the areas with black marker. Label North, South, East, and West.

4. Staple the community sketch to the board.

5. Add a caption naming your community.

Steps to Follow

1. Divide students into small groups and explain that they are going to create a 3-D community.

2. Refer to the "Places in Our Community" list made in preparation for the fold-out community project (page 83). Decide which buildings the class would like to depict on the bulletin board. Assign specific buildings to each group.

3. Students work together to create their assigned buildings. Cover boxes with construction paper and cut and paste important features so that the buildings resemble those in your community. (Be sure to put signs on the buildings.)

4. When buildings are completed, let each group tell the class about their buildings. Decide together where to place the buildings on the bulletin board.